BRAHMS

VARIATIONS ON A THEME OF HAYDN, OPP. 56A AND 56B

The Revised Scores of the Standard Editions

The Sketches · Textual Criticism and Notes

Historical Background · Analytical Essays

Views and Comments

NORTON CRITICAL SCORES

BACH CANTATA NO. 4
edited by Gerhard Herz

BACH CANTATA NO. 140
edited by Gerhard Herz

BEETHOVEN SYMPHONY NO. 5 IN C MINOR
edited by Elliot Forbes

BERLIOZ FANTASTIC SYMPHONY
edited by Edward T. Cone

BRAHMS VARIATIONS ON A THEME OF HAYDN, OPP. 56A AND 56B
edited by Donald M. McCorkle

CHOPIN PRELUDES, OPUS 28
edited by Thomas Higgins

DEBUSSY PRELUDE TO "THE AFTERNOON OF A FAUN"
edited by William W. Austin

HAYDN SYMPHONY NO. 103 IN E-FLAT MAJOR ("DRUM ROLL")
edited by Karl Geiringer

MOZART PIANO CONCERTO IN C MAJOR, K. 503
edited by Joseph Kerman

MOZART SYMPHONY IN G MINOR, K. 550
edited by Nathan Broder

PALESTRINA POPE MARCELLUS MASS
edited by Lewis Lockwood

SCHUBERT SYMPHONY IN B MINOR ("UNFINISHED")
edited by Martin Chusid

SCHUMANN DICHTERLIEBE
edited by Arthur Komar

STRAVINSKY PETRUSHKA
edited by Charles Hamm

A NORTON CRITICAL SCORE

Johannes Brahms

VARIATIONS ON A THEME OF HAYDN

FOR ORCHESTRA, OP. 56A AND FOR TWO PIANOS, OP. 56B

The Revised Scores of the Standard Editions
The Sketches · Textual Criticism and Notes
Historical Background · Analytical Essays
Views and Comments

Edited by

DONALD M. McCORKLE
THE UNIVERSITY OF BRITISH COLUMBIA

W · W · NORTON & COMPANY · INC · *New York*

FIRST EDITION

Library of Congress Cataloging in Publication Data

Brahms, Johannes, 1833–1897.
Variations on a theme of Haydn.

(Norton critical scores)
Bibliography: p.
1. Variations (Orchestra)—Scores. 2. Variations (Pianos (2)), Arranged. 3. Brahms, Johannes, 1833–1897. Variationen über ein Thema von Haydn, orchestra. I. Brahms, Johannes, 1833–1897. Variationen über ein Thema von Haydn; arr. 1976. II. McCorkle, Donald Macomber. III. Title. IV. Series.
M1003.B81op.56a 1976 76-21721
ISBN 0-393-02189-0
ISBN 0-393-09206-2 (pbk.)

PRINTED IN THE UNITED STATES OF AMERICA

1 2 3 4 5 6 7 8 9 0

Contents

Preface

The objective of this edition has been to produce the first comprehensive monograph on the *Variations on a Theme of Haydn* by Brahms, a masterpiece *sui generis* and a composition which established new precedents both in the history of music and in Brahms's stylistic development. What follows, accordingly, are two scores in the authoritative critical editions, together with a textual criticism, historical and theoretical analyses, and views and comments for illustrating the historical context, stylistic details, and significance of the work(s). Much of the factual information and essay material appears here for the first time in the English language. Two distinctive features of the edition are the inclusion of both the orchestral and two-piano versions of the *Haydn Variations* in the same volume, and the first publication of the complete sketches, which in juxtaposition may facilitate comparative studies of the two variant texts and a glimpse into the creative process of Brahms.

The scores are reproduced from Breitkopf & Härtel's *Johannes Brahms Sämtliche Werke,* edited by Hans Gál (Op. 56a) and Eusebius Mandyczewski (Op. 56b) for the Gesellschaft der Musikfreunde, Vienna, 1926–28. It has been necessary to make rather extensive revisions in the scores to rectify some important errors and missing details. I have undertaken to do so after collating all extant original scores, manuscripts, and editions in Vienna and Hamburg, including the two most valuable primary sources which were unavailable to the original editors. Their editorial work was thus somewhat incomplete insofar as they lacked the decisive evidence of Brahms's ultimate intentions, and so the *Haydn Variations* have been studied and performed for a half century from less than definitive editions. (Nevertheless, I have not found any of the other published editions to be as complete and reliable as the *Sämtliche Werke* editions.)

The sketches are reproduced in facsimile from the Brahms autograph and a portion are represented in my own transcription of the autograph. For permission to publish these most important of Brahms's sketches and a reproduction of the autograph score of the *Chorale St. Antoni* theme, also for the first time, I am very grateful to the Gesellschaft der Musikfreunde, and to Dr. Hedwig Mitringer, Archivist.

One might suppose that the *Haydn Variations* would be profusely commented upon in the Brahms literature, and that important analytical studies would be in abundance. But surprisingly, the relevant bibliography is no more than very slim at best. From the small amount of elucidating material which I have been able to find in the principal American, Austrian, and German libraries of Brahmsiana, I have selected analytical essays by four outstanding scholars representing different approaches to analysis, with views and comments by Brahms as well as several musicologists and critics who were close to him either personally or lineally. I am most indebted to Professor Murray J. Gould, who prepared a commentary on Schenker's analytic sketches expressly for this volume. My own written contributions attempt to reconstruct, narrate, and analyze the historical background and the sources, and to complement the other essays and commentaries. The selected bibliography includes the principal biographies of Brahms, the collected correspondence, the important studies relating to the *Haydn Variations* in particular, and to his variations in general.

I wish to express my appreciation to Professor Paul Henry Lang and Mr. David Hamilton for their interest which instigated this edition as a Norton Critical Score, and to Claire Brook, Music Editor, and Hinda Keller Farber of W. W. Norton & Company for their excellent guidance in seeing it through the stages of publication. My indebtedness is especially great to a number of music libraries and archives and their librarians for generous assistance during a necessarily protracted period of documentary research. I want to acknowledge in particular: The Library of Congress, Washington (Dr. Harold Spivacke, Messrs. Edward N. Waters, William Lichtenwanger, Rodney Mill, Jon Newsom, and Wayne Shirley); Gesellschaft der Musikfreunde, Vienna (Dr. Hedwig Mitringer); Österreichische Nationalbibliothek, Vienna (Dr. Leopold Nowak); Stadtbibliothek, Vienna (Dr. Fritz Racek); Staats- und Universitätsbibliothek, Hamburg (the late Dr. Kurt W. A. Richter, Dr. Bernhard Stockmann, and

Miss Helga Heim); and The University of British Columbia Music Library (Mr. Hans Burndorfer). To my good friend Mr. Kurt Hofmann, Hamburg, a dedicated collector and editor of Brahmsiana, I extend my thanks for several bibliographical favors over the course of a decade, and particularly for his courtesy in making available a photograph of his personal copy of the Vienna Philharmonic program for inclusion in this edition. And lastly, my deep appreciation to Dr. Hans Gál, who, as the book was going to press, graciously invited me to his home in Edinburgh and answered some of my questions about Brahms and the editorial procedures followed in preparing the *Sämtliche Werke*.

For my wife, Margit Lundstrom McCorkle, I reserve my deepest gratitude for her very important scholarly and artistic collaboration, which is impossible to acknowledge adequately. Specifically, she has been responsible for the bulk of the German-English translations prepared for this publication, and these include the often very abstruse expressions and involuted idiomatic syntax in the Brahms letters and in Max Kalbeck's monumental Brahms biography.

Finally, I wish to record my gratitude for several grants which have been indispensable aids to my work. The preliminary source research in Vienna was made possible to a large extent by a faculty award and sabbatical leave from the University of Maryland, College Park, in 1967 and 1971. The advanced stages of research, writing, and editing were accomplished during a research leave from The University of British Columbia in 1974–75. For the latter consideration I am most pleased to acknowledge my appreciation to Dean Robert M. Will, Faculty of Arts, for his sympathetic recognition of my need for precious time to bring the work to fruition. Some elusive final details were found while I was in Europe during the following summer on a research grant from The Canada Council.

DONALD M. MCCORKLE

The state of the s

(2) A supplying the second of the second

The State of the Market State of the

HISTORICAL BACKGROUND

On the Significance of the Haydn Variations

"What drove him toward the large forms was a longing for, an invincible attraction to, the great art of the German past and perhaps a desire to save it."

Paul Henry Lang

For the first work of Johannes Brahms represented in a Norton Critical Score, the reader may well ask why the *Variations on a Theme of Haydn* was chosen rather than one of the symphonies, concertos, solo piano or chamber works, or even *A German Requiem.* The answer to such a question is based on an assessment of this extraordinary composition by four criteria: as a work of art, as a landmark in Brahms's stylistic evolution, as a precedent in musical literature, and as tangible evidence for penetrating the arcana of his creative process.

The *Haydn Variations,*[1] in both the orchestral and two-piano versions, is a singular masterpiece, at once delightfully expressive and pro-

1. The original full titles are *Variationen über ein Thema von Jos. Haydn für Orchester von Johannes Brahms, Op. 56ª* and *Variationen über ein Thema von Joseph Haydn für zwei Pianoforte von Johannes Brahms, Op. 56ᵇ*, as printed by N. Simrock (Berlin, 1874 and 1873 respectively). In generally standardized American usage, the titles are most often translated as *Variations on a Theme of Haydn for Orchestra* and *for Two Pianos,* and abbreviated as *Haydn Variations.* The relatively recent British usage, *Variations on the St. Anthony Chorale* (and other variants), has no historical basis but was apparently coined as a solution to the problem of disputed authorship by Haydn of the *Chorale St. Antoni* theme. Since modern scholarship has not yet conclusively settled the question of authorship, it is only reasonable to retain the original titles (and their literal translation) as modified. The problem of the source of the theme is considered in more detail on pages 27–30.

foundly organized, whose elements are balanced to a degree unusual even for Brahms. Indeed, it is so subtly integrated that the auditory impression it conveys fairly masks the complex structural details permeating the musical substance. How very slightly are casual listeners made aware of the perfection in the use of variational, textural, and idiomatic concepts in this work, which seems to make relatively few intellectual demands for its appreciation. But the simplicity is illusory, for it is a compendium in microcosm—the most distilled essence, as it were—of the compositional craft and musical aesthetics of Brahms, as well as a phenomenal artistic amalgam of Baroque, Classical, and Romantic formal and stylistic components.

Among earlier commentators, it became almost a commonplace that the *Haydn Variations* was given attention primarily as a prelude to, or an immediate precursor of, the four symphonies. Although chronologically and stylistically correct, this emphasis has tended to eclipse the intrinsic worth of the work in its own right. The orchestral variations, as Walter Niemann observed, were ". . . already the first truly symphonic work of Brahms . . . [they] belong not only to the most erudite, but also to the most outwardly brilliant, effective and diversified [compositions] of the Master. Certainly in invention, they belong to Brahms's freshest and richest works."[2] The two-piano version, conversely, has rarely been more than passingly mentioned by other writers, who thus have overlooked its priority as the original conception. In itself, this coequal version, unadorned by orchestral color, is more transparent texturally than its dominant twin and therefore better able to disclose the wealth of melodic, harmonic, and rhythmic invention in the contrapuntal fabric so finely and felicitously wrought by Brahms.

Audiences have continued to hear the orchestral variations rather frequently since the first performance in 1873, because the work rightfully maintains an important place in the repertoire. The two-piano version, however, which found its way into the literature somewhat later (the first performance may have been by Hans von Bülow and Charles Hallé in Manchester, February 12, 1874),[3] has never enjoyed such wide

2. Walter Niemann, *Brahms* (Berlin, 1920), pp. 271–72.

3. The actual date and circumstances of the premiere have not been ascertained, to my knowledge. However, it is possible that the performance announced by von Bülow in a letter of Jan. 23, 1874 (*Hans von Bülow Briefe und Schriften,* 8 vols., ed. Marie von Bülow [Leipzig, 1895–1908], V, p. 135) may well have been the first public performance. In the following year (1875) Clara Schumann added it to her repertoire.

currency, though it remains one of the monuments in the repertoire of duo-pianists.

Brahms himself often included the *Haydn Variations* in his own concerts as guest conductor of various orchestras and very likely played the two-piano version privately with friends. He once spoke of his special affection for the latter in a letter to Clara Schumann, when he said, "I have always had a weakness for that piece and I think of it with more pleasure and satisfaction than of many another."[4] She undoubtedly shared his enthusiasm, as did von Bülow, for they both performed it with various partners for many years and (according to their letters) to much acclaim.

Historically, the *Haydn Variations* was a pivotal work, marking a transition point in Brahms's development from impressionable young Romanticist to maturity as a classicistic Romanticist. It was, moreover, the culmination of his efforts as a composer of independent variations and large-scale piano works, as well as his introduction of a new genre, the first set of independent variations for orchestra in the history of music.[5] This remarkable synthesis of the Romanticists' miniature character piece and Beethoven's type of character variations climaxed in a Bachian passacaglia, the first time a basso-ostinato construction was used to conclude a set of character variations.[6] (Basso ostinato variations appeared again thirteen years later in the finale of the *Fourth Symphony*.)

Whether Brahms knew how advanced his achievement was we can only conjecture. But he was probably aware of the historical precedents, for he was as well informed as any composer of the age about his heritage. As a student and practitioner of the several variation techniques he was a specialist. His disdain for the currently fashionable ornamental (or *fantasia*) variations—with which he himself had had experience in his youth—and his great reverence for the earlier variation procedures was expressed several times in letters to his friends.[7] He held as his ideals the *Goldberg Variations* of Bach and the *Diabelli Variations* of Beethoven,[8]

4. Letter (March 15, 1891), *Letters of Clara Schumann and Johannes Brahms, 1853–1896*, ed. Berthold Litzmann, 2 vols (London, 1927), II, p. 189.

5. Robert U. Nelson, *The Technique of Variation. A Study of the Instrumental Variation Form from Antonio de Cabezón to Max Reger* (Berkeley and Los Angeles, 1948), p. 175.

6. Nelson, *op. cit.*, p. 108.

7. See, for example, his comment given on page 216 of this volume.

8. It is further enlightening to see that his collection of Beethoven piano variations included original or early editions not only of the *33 Variations on a Waltz by*

so it is not surprising that stylistic influences of both masters appear in the final set of variations of the last great master of the genre.

Finally, the *Haydn Variations* is essential for providing a rare glimpse into Brahms's compositional workshop. For this is a unique composition, existing not only in two separate versions for entirely different media—and thus as distinct works with individual integrity (one of the two times Brahms evidently regarded two versions as equals)—but also in a set of sketches which are the sole extensive preliminary drafts he retained and bequeathed to posterity. Of course, the variations must also be considered (with the two string quartets, Op. 51, and the orchestration of three *Hungarian Dances* in the same year) as one of the final steps toward his *First Symphony*. We may infer that he was inspired by his attainment of a successful integration of style, expression, and orchestration to break out of the psychological restraints which had kept him from moving ahead with the symphony, already in gestation for some years.

In the following three sections the significance of the *Haydn Variations* will be examined further in three aspects of the historical background: first, a biographical sketch of Brahms in personal and artistic transition within the perspective of his changing Viennese ambience; second, a focus on these variations in the context of his portfolio of concurrent works; and third, an analytical study of his creative process as seen through comparison of the sketches and two versions.

Diabelli (Op. 120), but also of the following: *32 Variations on an Original Theme* (WoO 80), *6 Variations in F Major* (Op. 34), *15 Variations in E-flat and Fugue ("Eroica,"* Op. 35), *13 Variations on the Ariette "Es war einmal ein alter Mann" by Dittersdorf* (WoO 66), *8 Variations on a Theme by Waldstein* (WoO 67), as well as variations for piano and string instruments. See Alfred Orel, "Johannes Brahms' Musikbibliothek," *N. Simrock Jahrbuch III,* ed. Erich H. Müller (Leipzig, 1930/34), pp. 28–29. Reprinted in Kurt Hofmann, *Die Bibliothek von Johannes Brahms; Bücher und Musikalienverzeichnis* (Hamburg, 1974), pp. 147–48.

Brahms and Vienna in Transition, 1869-73

When Johannes Brahms (1833–97) left Vienna in the spring of 1873 for his annual four-month composing retreat and vacation, he had passed his first decade of residence in the Austrian capital and completed his first year of three as artistic director of the Gesellschaft der Musikfreunde (Society of Friends of Music), one of the most prestigious positions of Viennese musical culture. Moreover and most significantly, as he approached his fortieth birthday, he stood almost at the mid-point of his career as the foremost classicist of the post-Beethovenian Romantic Era.[1] He had in fact reached a crest in his twenty years as a composer, and fairly fulfilled the extravagant prophecy of his ultimate ascendancy made by Robert Schumann, his mentor, two decades earlier.[2]

His expanding catalogue by 1873 consisted of chamber and orchestral works, sonatas, variations, and character pieces for piano, choral works, and some ninety-six songs. Included within these published fifty-six *opera* and assorted works without opus number were such masterpieces as the

1. The bulk of biographical and historical information about Brahms and his work is contained chiefly in two sets of published sources: Max Kalbeck, *Johannes Brahms,* 4 vols. in 8 (Berlin, 1908–14) and the *Johannes Brahms Briefwechsel,* 16 vols. (Berlin, 1908–22; repr. Tutzing, 1974). The best biographies in English are Florence May, *The Life of Johannes Brahms,* 2 vols. (London, 1905; 2nd ed. [ca. 1948?]), and Karl Geiringer, *Brahms; His Life and Work,* 2nd ed. (Garden City, 1961).

2. Schumann's article "Neue Bahnen" (New Paths), his last for *Die Neue Zeitschrift für Musik,* 1853, has been published in translation in a number of books, among them Oliver Strunk, *Source Readings in Music History* (New York, 1950), pp. 844–45; paperback edition, *Source Readings in Music History: The Romantic Era* (1965), pp. 104–05.

Piano Trio, Op. 8 (first version); *Piano Concerto in D minor; Sextet in B-flat Major,* Op. 18; *Variations and Fugue on a Theme of Handel;* two *Piano Quartets,* Opp. 25 and 26; *Magelone Romances,* Op. 33; *Piano Quintet,* Op. 34; *Variations on a Theme of Paganini; Ein deutsches Requiem; Liebeslieder Walzes,* Op. 52; *Alto Rhapsody,* Op. 53; and more than two dozen exquisite lieder and songs.[3] With the publication of his crowning achievement in choral composition, *Ein deutsches Requiem* (1869), and the extraordinary reception accorded it during the next several years throughout Germanic Europe and England, Brahms's fame and primacy in all genres but symphony and opera were virtually secured.[4]

The five-year period surrounding the appearance of the *Requiem* was evidently a time of preoccupation with the vocal idiom. For aside from the *Liebeslieder Waltzes* (1869), which were conceived for piano four-hands "and singing *ad libitum,*" and the *Sonata,* Op.34*bis* (1871 or 1872), which was composed some years earlier, Brahms produced a prodigious amount of vocal and choral music; some seventy-six lieder and other songs with piano accompaniment and four concerted quasi cantatas, *Rinaldo* (1869), *Alto Rhapsody* (1869?), *Schicksalslied* (1871), and *Triumphlied* (1872). Not since 1866 had he published new instrumental compositions—though some were being sketched and drafted—to add to those which had appeared in a spate in that one year.

The year between the autumns of 1872 and 1873 can therefore be viewed in retrospect as a transitional phase from the long hiatus in instrumental composition. During this year Brahms was taking measured steps toward his long-deferred goals, the string quartet and the symphony—the ultimate achievements for, in Alfred Einstein's phrase, "the greatest representative of the musical Romantic movement, which sought to come to terms creatively with the past, unable to disregard Bach and Handel, Haydn and Mozart, and—above all Beethoven."[5] In short, the early 1870s

3. The most recent reliable thematic catalogue of his works to be published is an unabridged reprint of the *Simrock Brahms Verzeichniss* of 1897: *The N. Simrock Thematic Catalog of the Works of Johannes Brahms,* with a new introduction, including addenda and corrigenda, by Donald M. McCorkle (New York, 1973).

4. In the United States his recognition came several decades later, especially from the impetus given by the then young orchestras, under German and Austrian conductors, in New York, Boston, Chicago, Philadelphia, etc. The New York performance in 1855 of his *Trio,* Op. 8, by Theodore Thomas, Carl Bergmann, and William Mason—which was also the world premiere—was as much a rarity as the 1862 performance by Bergmann and the New York Philharmonic of his *Second Serenade,* Op. 16 (1860 edition).

5. *Music In The Romantic Era* (New York, 1947), p. 150.

generally, and 1873 particularly, were for Brahms a critical turning point, intellectually and psychologically, during which he moved in the direction of fulfillment as a master of the large abstract forms. The completion of the *Variations on a Theme of Haydn* (in both versions) and the *Two String Quartets,* Op. 51, in the summer of 1873 marked the end of his transition to symphonist.

Thus was 1873 a vintage year for Brahms as a composer. As we shall see, however, his artistic successes were to be achieved in the midst of an atmosphere of extraordinary turmoil and tension because of momentous events in Vienna and a serious strain in relations with his two oldest friends, Clara Schumann (1819–96) and Joseph Joachim (1831–1907). Both of these external conditions, as a confrontation between the present and the past, could not fail to exert their influence on his sensitive creative psyche.

The period of the early seventies was a notable turning point in the Viennese socio-cultural milieu.[6] In recent years the compromise creation of the Dual Monarchy of Austria and Hungary had effectively weakened the political hegemony and prestige of the Austrian state, while inevitably strengthening the demands of its citizens for greater freedom of thought and speech. At the same time, the Viennese bourgeoisie, in an exuberant mood of optimism, launched an orgy of reckless financial speculation and lavish spending to celebrate their euphoria, which was to culminate in catastrophic events and fundamental changes in the order and style of Viennese life. The pivotal year, 1873, was at once the peak of the financial boom, the occasion of the fabulous Vienna World Exhibition which attracted millions of visitors but ended in financial disaster for the investors, and the ultimate crash of the stock exchange which effected every segment of the population and sent shock waves around the world.

The depression which ensued gave justification to the state to accelerate construction and architectural modernization of the city as a mitigation for the despondency of the populace. The result was that the Ringstrasse, the spectacular circumferential boulevard begun in the previous decade over the demolished ancient ramparts, acquired neo-Renaissance, neo-Gothic, and neo-Hellenistic buildings in steady succession throughout

6. A good English-language survey of this era is contained in Ilsa Barea, *Vienna* (New York, 1967), chapter 5. Certain aspects of the essence of Vienna's atmosphere are sketched in Joseph Wechsberg, *Vienna, My Vienna* (New York, 1968).

the seventies, until the original city of Baroque palaces was surrounded by monumental state museums, theaters, and other public buildings to symbolize the power, wealth, and dignity of the declining Habsburg Empire.

The central edifice in this eclectic mélange was the magnificent Court Opera House, replacing the old Kärntnertor Theater as the principal opera theater in imperial and royal Vienna.[7] With its opening in 1869, the historic operamania of the Viennese could be focused and accommodated for the first time in one great house, and the gargantuan stage, orchestra pit, and acoustical demands of Richard Wagner could be realized. Vienna thus became the pre-Bayreuth home of the Wagner opera cult, a phenomenon which coincided with and symbolized the radically changing social structure and artistic taste of the Viennese. The Wagner-mania, as Eduard Hanslick saw it, was only a step short of the status of a "Dalai Lama cult."[8]

The year 1873 also marked a momentous shift in the other arts. Almost simultaneously, as it happened, the two foremost Germanic painters of the period came to artistic collision in Vienna, and the manifestations were long lasting. The first of them was Hans Makart (1840–84),[9] a Salzburger who had been brought to Vienna by Emperor Franz Josef in 1869 to become an instant sensation. Makart's extraordinary career was vastly propelled by two timely works produced in 1873: a gigantic oil painting for the World Exhibition, *Venice Pays Homage to Caterina Cornaro,* and a complete interior decoration for a whole room in the Ringstrasse mansion of Nikolaus Dumba, the industrialist. These works, in their erotically vivid colors, theatrical opulence, and feminine sensuality, were grandiose to an extreme and fully exalted the taste of the *nouveaux riches* of Viennese society. As a result, the whole Ringstrasse era came to be called also "the age of Makart" and "the age of the *parvenu.*" Within a short space of time the Makart style of total interior decoration—luxuriant exhibitionism, "historical" allegories, opulent hangings, picturesque

7. See Marcel Prawy, *The Vienna Opera* (New York, 1969), for a history of opera in Vienna.

8. Hanslick, *Die moderne Oper. Kritiken und Studien,* 4th ed. (Berlin, 1880), p. 322.

9. See *Hans Makart; Triumph einer schönen Epoche,* ed. Klaus Gallwitz, Makart-Ausstellung, Staatliche Kunsthalle (Baden-Baden, 1972): an exhibition catalogue together with important essays on the life and work of Makart. See also *Hans Makart, Entwürfe und Phantasien,* ed. Gerbert Frodl and Renata Mikula (Vienna, 1975): an exhibition catalogue of Makart's preliminary sketches, including reproductions, descriptive matter, and commentary.

objets d'art, potted palms, oriental fans, and the like—permeated elegant homes and swept away all but vestiges of the traditional Baroque and Biedermeier decor.[10]

The other painter, the complete antithesis to Makart and Makartism, was Anselm Feuerbach (1829–80),[11] the outstanding German exponent of neo-classicism. Feuerbach was called to Vienna to become professor of historical painting at the Academy of Fine Arts. By all odds, it was an ill-fated appointment at this time and place for an artist whose antiquarian subjects were essentially linear and plastic, precise in rhythm, counterpoint, and detail, but austere in color and aloof in emotion. It is clear that Brahms felt a keen aesthetic affinity with Feuerbach, in that he acquired copies of most, if not all, of his works, kept in contact through their mutual friend, the art engraver and photographer Julius Allgeyer of Munich, and was inspired by Feuerbach to write both the *Alto Rhapsody* and *Nänie.*[12] But Brahms took pains (at the cost of further friendship) to caution the high-strung and fragile painter against being too optimistic about the reception of his enormous painting in the World Exhibition.[13] Feuerbach resentfully ignored Brahms's counsel and was ultimately vilified by the Viennese for his *Battle of the Amazons.*[14]

Within this panorama of exuberant and volatile confusion, and at the time when the artistic tastes of the ambitious middle class were superseding those of the upper-class circles, Brahms was making a place for himself in the great polyglot cosmopolis on the Danube. The Viennese musical establishment—controlled in the main by Germanophiles—had accepted him readily as a performing musician, but only more gradually as a composer, since his arrival in 1862. At the outset of his residency Brahms had made no plans to settle down permanently, preferring to find a conductorial post in one of the German cities—ideally in Hamburg—which he continued to hope would be forthcoming. However, as

10. Even Dr. Billroth, Brahms's best friend and a man of patrician taste and cultivation, ultimately decorated his famous music room to conform to the current taste.

11. See Julius Allgeyer, *Anselm Feuerbach; Sein Leben und seine Kunst* (Bamberg, 1894) or Hermann Uhde-Bernays, ed., *Feuerbach; Des Meisters Gemälde in 200 Abbildungen* (Stuttgart & Berlin, 1913).

12. According to Kalbeck (*op. cit.,* II/2, pp. 305–06), Brahms was reminded of Feuerbach by the character Plessing in Goethe's *Harzreise im Winter* and so composed the *Alto Rhapsody,* Op. 53, as a symbolic biographical and psychological sketch of the painter. The later *Nänie,* Op. 82, was written as a memorial to Feuerbach and dedicated to his stepmother, Henriette Feuerbach, in 1881.

13. Kalbeck, *op. cit.,* II/2, p. 422.

14. Reproduced in both Uhde-Bernays, *op. cit.,* p. 161, and H. Bodmer, *Feuerbach* (Leipzig, 1942), p. 94.

the years passed and some attractive offers came, he eventually admitted (in 1869) that he could not be pried away from Vienna because he had the most desirable environment for his art to prosper, so he made peace with himself and established permanent residence.

Fortunately, he was developing both the financial means (through his publications) and life-style to protect himself from occupational burdens and extraneous disruptions which would interfere with his single-minded professional and personal pursuits. In effect, he had reached the enviable situation of being able to do just what he wished with his energy and time. His work pattern was generally fixed, with winters in Vienna where he drafted new compositions, made revisions, and read galley proofs, and with summers in idyllic mountain and lake villages in Germany, Austria, and Switzerland, where he found the inspiration and tranquility to complete his major works.

Already at the beginning of the seventies Brahms was widely regarded (and promoted by the anti-Wagnerites all over Europe) as one of the two living "Masters" of German music. He thus became in every way the antithesis to Wagner, his senior by twenty years, and the fanatic Wagnerites, who increasingly reviled him with slander and innuendo in proportion to his growing stature. Consequently he represented the champion of the traditional aesthetic ideals to the conservative intelligentsia who abhorred the musical, social, and political implications of the Wagnerian revolution. To what extent the mounting crescendo of the Wagner-Brahms hostilities may have caused Brahms's rather sudden intensification of his inherent classicistic impulses probably cannot be known. However, it is clear that around 1873 he did consciously shift his stylistic emphasis away from a Schumannesque to a more Beethovenian Romanticism,[15] as if compelled to objectify the embodiment of tradition in musical craft and aesthetics that his friends and devotees held him to be. At the same time, some of his music was actually achieving wide acceptance, notwithstanding the gravity of his style, which evoked a recurring refrain from unsympathetic performers, audiences, and critics complaining of "diffuseness," "abstruseness," "intellectualism," and "lack of

15. Geiringer (*op. cit.*, pp. 211–12) pinpoints the essence of this stylistic change as follows: "And when at last, in the summer of 1873, he completed the *String Quartets in C minor and A minor,* Op. 51, he had not only conquered a new form of ensemble, but at the same time his style developed to its full maturity. He had now achieved an economy which refused to tolerate a single superfluous note, but at the same time he had perfected a method of integration that would give an entire work the appearance of having been cast from one mold."

originality" and alleging even more basic faults.[16] Inevitably, of course, it was his lighter and more generally accessible music—*Hungarian Dances,* the Op. 39 *Waltzes, Liebeslieder Waltzes, Deutsche Volkslieder* —which brought him most immediate popularity among the sentimental Viennese in this frivolous age of *Gemütlichkeit,* the era of "wine, women, and song" glorified by Johann Strauss the Younger, in his waltzes and operettas.[17]

The artistic focus for Brahms was the Gesellschaft der Musikfreunde, which had also built a new building in 1869 to accommodate better the society's venerable enterprises, the *Orchesterverein* (Orchestral Society), *Singverein* (Choral Society), *Conservatorium* (predecessor of the Academy of Music), and valuable library and archives. The new building was located immediately outside the Ringstrasse, a few blocks from the Court Opera House. The Gesellschaft was then (and for many years thereafter) the center of Viennese concert activity and a bastion of conservatism under the long-term directorship of Johann Herbeck.[18] In the autumn of 1872, Brahms was appointed artistic director, which placed him in charge of choral and orchestral concerts during three years (1872–75). His success in the directorship—which at the same time was to be his last position—was marked by two notable achievements: reorganization of the amateur orchestra by replacing the weaker members with professionals from the Court Opera Orchestra and strengthening the choral activities by introducing better repertoire and rehearsal procedures.[19] The first season set the standard of Brahms's programming ideals and was by and large an artistically successful series of seven concerts of symphonies, overtures, arias and songs, cantatas, chorales, and the like. His choice of composers was indicative of his taste: Handel, Mozart, Eccard, Isaac, Schubert, Gluck, J. S. Bach, Hiller, Schumann, Mendelssohn, Haydn, Beethoven, Cherubini, and Brahms. Included in the programs were the

16. Such pejorative views can be gleaned from contemporary newspaper reviews; see for example the selection in Nicolas Slonimsky, *Lexicon of Musical Invective* (New York, 1965), pp. 68–79.

17. Significantly, Brahms was on friendly terms with the dazzling "Waltz King" and genuinely loved *Die Fledermaus* (1874) and many of the lilting waltzes. Strauss later dedicated the waltzes *Seid umschlungen Millionen,* Op. 433, to Brahms.

18. Herbeck was also the man who introduced Schubert's *Symphony in B minor* ("Unfinished") in 1865. In 1870 he resigned from the Gesellschaft to become director of the Court Opera (until 1875). He was succeeded at the Gesellschaft by the Russian composer and pianist Anton Rubinstein (1829–94) for one year, who gave up the post to Brahms. Herbeck took back the position from Brahms in 1875.

19. Geiringer, *op. cit.,* p. 103.

Viennese premieres of his own *Triumphlied* (Song of Triumph on the Victory of German Arms), written in tribute to the Prussians, and Handel's oratorio *Saul*.[20]

Apart from his professional life, and although he had a complex personality, Brahms's physical and emotional needs had never really progressed very far beyond the relative rusticity of a North German lower-middle-class burgher. His personal Vienna was the inner city, where the fading architectural glories of the Italo-Austrian Baroque crowded the narrow and winding streets with attractions for all the senses. His favorite haunts near the cathedral were the restaurant "Zum Roten Igel" (At the Red Hedgehog), and the "Gauses Pilsener Bier Halle," where he joined the so-called "table society" of influential journalists, scholars, and artists for good drink and informal colloquia.[21] Brahms was well known in Vienna as an indefatigable walker in all seasons; from his spartan bachelor's apartment across the street from the great Carlskirche he customarily made a daily trek of several miles through the city for his meals, wine, and coffee. And like most good Viennese he often crossed the Danube Canal for promenades and outings in that wonderful park, the Prater. But surely the pervading intangible attraction of the city for him was the fact—which he often mentioned—that this had been the spiritual home of music and great musicians for several centuries, and in particular, of his heroes Beethoven, Schubert, and Mozart.

All the while, Brahms was developing a coterie of good friends in Vienna, which, as it grew, became an extraordinary aggregate of professional musicians, musical and literary scholars, physicians, writers, and critics who empathized with the man and his music. These friendships were all the more remarkable in view of Brahms's essentially solitary nature and difficult personality, which became more pronounced as he matured. His closest friends at this time were Dr. Theodor Billroth (1829–94),[22] the foremost surgeon in Europe and a cultivated musical dilettante,

20. Several of the year's programs are quoted in May, *op. cit.*, II, pp. 466–71.

21. Kalbeck, *op. cit.*, II/2, pp. 423–28.

22. Billroth, during nearly three decades as professor of surgery at the University of Vienna, became one of the world's greatest surgeons through his brilliant research, technical innovations, and teaching. At that time the Vienna medical faculty was probably at the peak of excellence in its history. Dr. Billroth's prodigious intellectual energy as a scientist could only be balanced, however, by a passion for music which he cultivated assiduously. His 18th-century mansion was the hub of the Viennese Brahms circle for a quarter century. It can be said in truth that the great physician participated actively in the creation of many of the Brahms masterpieces, for most of the new compositions from ca. 1867 were submitted by Brahms for Billroth's criticism and previewed in the Billroth *Musikabende* before public performance and publication. Billroth himself was the dedicatee of the *Two String Quartets*, Op. 51.

and Eduard Hanslick (1825–1904),[23] music critic of the *Neue freie Presse,* formidable antagonist of Wagner, and first professor of the history and aesthetics of music at the university. These two genial men never wavered in their devotion to Brahms. Others in the circle included Gustav Nottebohm (1817–82), the Beethoven scholar; Carl Ferdinand Pohl (1819–87), the Haydn specialist and librarian of the Gesellschaft der Musikfreunde; the composers Ignaz Brüll (1846–1907) and Carl Goldmark (1830–1915); the pianist and teacher Julius Epstein (1832–1926); and from the Court Opera, the conductors Otto Dessoff (1835–92) and Johann Herbeck (1831–77) and the leading soprano and tenor, Luise Dustmann-Meyer (1831–99) and Gustav Walter (1834–1910).

Several crises in Brahms's personal relations arose during the late winter and early spring of 1873 when he found himself twice embroiled in controversies over plans for his possible participation in festival performances.[24] Of the two, the second controversy, which resulted from some hapless moves by the committee charged with developing a Schumann Memorial Festival to be held in Bonn in mid-August, affected him much more deeply because it strained his relations with Clara Schumann and Joseph Joachim. As the festival plans progressed throughout the winter, Brahms grew simultaneously less definite in expressing his wishes for his own anticipated role and more perverse in his attitude toward the planning committee, Joachim (who was one of the two codirectors), and Clara. The ensuing confusion revolved around the committee's desire that Brahms write a new choral work expressly for the occasion and Joachim's wish for a performance of *Ein deutsches Requiem,* conducted by Brahms, which would be especially appropriate for a Schumann memorial concert. The progressively more complicated misunderstandings that followed seemed somewhat resolved by the end of April, when Joachim wrote to say that the committee had reached a compromise and that he wished to ask Brahms to conduct the *Requiem,* and ". . . something further would be delightful, namely, if besides the direction of the *Requiem,* you would also play the two-piano variations with

23. See page 211 of this volume.

24. The first of these involved preparations for special concerts to open the Vienna World Exhibition in May, at which the *Singverein* was expected to perform. There followed a series of vexatious meetings with the planning committee during which the idea of repeating a recent highly successful *Singverein* program was replaced by a grandiose plan for an all-Schubert program under Brahms's direction. He opposed the new plan as impractical and, since he was under no contractual obligation after the season, withdrew in disappointment and relief.

Frau Clara at the chamber-music morning [concert]."[25] But it is obvious that Brahms and Joachim were still not communicating clearly and Brahms was balking when he concluded this phase of the episode with his enigmatic response to Joachim: "Now perhaps the variations for two pianos are better omitted, in case I do not conduct?"[26]

This exchange with Joachim coincided with Brahms's frustrations over failure to find a satisfactory summer retreat in the Styrian Alps, to take the place of Baden-Baden, the Black Forest spa, where it had been his custom for a decade to spend his summers near Clara Schumann. Thus at loose ends and disconcerted, he returned to Vienna and immediately made up his mind to go westward to Munich. Once there he called upon his friends Hermann Levi, *Kapellmeister* of the Court Opera, and Julius Allgeyer for their help in finding a retreat in the area. They introduced him to the charming resort village of Tutzing on the Starnberger See, a short train trip southwest of the Bavarian capital. His residence for the spring and summer (to last from mid-May to mid-September) was a comfortable inn situated only moments from the walking path along the lake and the center of the picturesque town.

His pleasure was expressed after getting settled, in a letter to Levi:

> Tutzing is far more beautiful than we could imagine the other day.
>
> We just had a magnificent thunderstorm, the lake was almost black, along the shores splendidly green; for usually it is blue, yet more beautiful, deeper blue than the sky. In addition, the range of snow-covered mountains—one cannot see one's fill.
>
> But unfortunately, one feels more often the need to puff into the face of the beautiful scenery. When you come [down], I should like you to bring along some French, or better, Turkish tobacco for cigarettes. Writing verse and music would certainly seem an almost lighter offense [then].[27]

And so, having secured his usual requities for achieving spiritual tranquility and relieving the tensions of intellectual labor, he was ready to get back to work.

25. *Johannes Brahms Briefwechsel,* VI, pp. 79–80; translation by the editor. In alluding to "the two-piano variations" Joachim was evidently speaking of Robert Schumann's *Andante and Variations,* Op. 46, for two pianos, rather than Brahms's *Haydn Variations,* of which he probably had no advance knowledge.

26. *Ibid.*, p. 80. However, the *Andante and Variations* remained in the program and was performed by Clara Schumann and Ernst Rudorff (Berthold Litzmann, *Clara Schumann, Ein Künstlerleben nach Tagebüchern und Briefen,* 3 vols. [Leipzig, 1902, 1905, 1908], III, p. 29).

27. *Johannes Brahms Briefwechsel,* VII, p. 134; translation by the editor. A typical instance of Brahms's often obscure prose, which can make easy comprehension impossible for the noninitiated.

The Variations within the 1873 Portfolio

Brahms must have laid out his quota of work for these months to consist primarily of three projects, two large and one small: (1) the completion from sketches of the *Haydn Variations* for two pianos[1] (and subsequently the transcription for orchestra); (2) extensive revisions, if not a general recasting, of the long-awaited first two string quartets, which had existed in some form or other since the summer of 1869; and (3) the completion of a new set of lieder, to be published in two books as the *Lieder und Gesänge,* Op. 59.[2] A rather formidable goal this must have been, considering Brahms's customary daily schedule of about four hours of work balanced with long walks, reading, leisurely dining, and making music and relaxing with his friends.

Clearly, May and June were a period of diligent creative effort, devoted to intensive work on his three projects, all of which were probably carried on concurrently. It is impossible to know exactly how much effort was required because of Brahms's usually very successful penchant for keeping historical and biographical details of his compositional activity close to his vest. We may be certain only that the set of eight lieder was

1. The sketches are not and probably cannot be dated, so it is impossible to determine how much of the work was roughed out before he went to Tutzing. This question is considered further on pages 36 ff.

2. The nonconsecutive numbering of these new *opera* (i.e., Opp. 51, 56, 59) is explained by Brahms's having reserved Op. 51 in anticipation of earlier completion of the quartet(s), and his confusion in thinking that all of the opus numbers between 52 and 58 already had been assigned! Op. 56 was therefore discovered to be an unassigned gap to be filled. (*Johannes Brahms Briefwechsel,* 16 vols. [Berlin, 1908–22; repr. Tutzing, 1974], IX, p. 123.)

more than half completed before he left Vienna in April,[3] the variations (for two pianos) were finished sometime in July, after which primary attention was shifted to the quartets for virtual completion by the end of August.[4] Brahms himself tells us about the variations and the quartets, albeit obliquely, in the fair-copy autograph (*Reinschrift*) of the *Haydn Variations* and in a letter to Dr. Billroth, both of which were dated simply July 1873. The letter,[5] couched in characteristic Brahmsian irony and puns reserved for his best friends, says that "a volume of immensely difficult piano variations" was ready as an alternative offering, should Billroth not wish to accept the dedication of a new string quartet which was in the offing.[6]

It was well that the bulk of his compositional labor was completed before a succession of friends dropped in to visit him and the tourists began their annual swarm to Tutzing in July. In the meantime, he was also making frequent trips to Munich to visit Levi, Allgeyer and a number of other friends and acquaintances, including Levi's colleague Franz Wüllner, the senior Court *Kapellmeister,* the poet Paul Heyse (1830–14), with whom Brahms was considering possible collaboration on an opera, and a certain Lucie Coster, a Dutch piano student from Java whose company he found pleasurable and amusing. The primary objective of these excursions, however, was the opportunity to have trial readings of the evolving quartets with the Joseph Walter String Quartet

3. He had in fact mailed manuscript copies of four songs (*Regenlied, Nachklang, Mein wundes Herz, Dein blaues Auge*), to the poet, Claus Groth (1819–99), prior to April 20th (received by Groth in Kiel and acknowledged on April 20 [*Briefe der Freundschaft. Johannes Brahms-Klaus Groth,* ed. Volquart Pauls (Heide, 1956), p. 74]); and the first song in the set (*Damm'rung senkte sich von Oben* by Goethe) had lain around since 1870 or 1871. So we may be reasonably sure that his attention was devoted to three songs only: *Auf dem See* (Carl Simrock), *Agnes* (Mörike), and *Eine gute Nacht* (G. F. Daumer); but naturally the possibility cannot be overlooked that some time was given to revising the other five songs to complete the collective opus. (Max Kalbeck [*Johannes Brahms,* 4 vols. in 8 (Berlin, 1908–14), II/2, pp. 377–78] was surely in error in believing that seven of the eight songs were written in Tutzing.) Brahms had the good fortune to become acquainted with two singers of Tutzing, Heinrich and Therese Vogl (the "Tristan and Isolde" of the Munich Opera), who gave him valuable assistance by trying out his new songs in private readings.

4. The chronology of work in this time period is by no means firmly established; however, it can be reconstructed to some extent by deduction from relevant references in Kalbeck (*ibid., passim*) and the *Johannes Brahms Briefwechsel* (*passim*).

5. *Billroth im Briefwechsel mit Brahms,* ed. Otto Gottlieb-Billroth (Munich & Berlin, 1964), pp. 43–44.

6. Actually, both quartets, Op. 51, were ultimately dedicated to Billroth after Brahms, in a mood of pique with Joachim over the Schumann Festival, decided not to dedicate Op. 51, No. 2 to Joachim.

and to have them criticized by his friends, a usual stage in his creative process. He did not similarly expose the *Haydn Variations* to his Munich friends, or so we may infer from the lack of mention in his collected correspondence with Levi and Allgeyer. In fact, it appears that he was especially secretive about this composition, and one can therefore speculate that it was being kept under wraps as a surprise for Clara Schumann, under whose inspiration he had composed the *Handel Variations* twelve years earlier.[7] Allgeyer was perhaps the first to see the *Haydn Variations,* when Brahms wrote him early in August to request a copyist for the "enclosed trash" which had to be finished before the 14th.[8]

On the 14th Brahms did after all take a train to Bonn to attend the Schumann Festival (August 17–19) of orchestral and chamber music, which was organized to raise money toward a grave memorial to Robert Schumann. Clara Schumann naturally was an active participant, but Brahms did not perform, nor was the *Requiem* given. The whole mishandled episode had reached a peak in July when Brahms read in a newspaper that the *Requiem* was being dropped from the program, though the *Neue Zeitschrift für Musik,* as late as the May 16th issue, announced that the *Requiem* would open the Festival.[9] One can therefore understand something of Brahms's disappointment and consequent testiness during the festivities, which was mitigated only by the presence of other old musician friends in the audience.

The day after the Festival ended, Brahms and Clara[10] played

7. It was Brahms's custom for many years to dedicate and/or present a new composition to Clara on her birthday (September 13). Piano variations were especially highly regarded among these gifts. Such was the *Handel Variations* in 1861, which, on the penultimate draft (but not the printed edition) given to Clara, Brahms inscribed "Variationen / für eine liebe Freundin. / Aria di Händel || Johs. Brahms. Sept: 61." (Present owner, The Library of Congress, Washington [No. ML 30.8b.B7 Op. 24 Case].) Previously, he had dedicated to her the *Variations on a Theme of Robert Schumann,* Op. 9 (1854), and in 1860 the variations which were to become the *Andante* movement of the *Sextet,* Op. 18.

8. Alfred Orel, ed., *Johannes Brahms und Julius Allgeyer; Eine Künstlerfreundschaft in Briefen* (Tutzing, 1964), p. 95.

9. *Neue Zeitschrift für Musik,* Leipzig, May 16, 1873, p. 223.

10. Clara Schumann, at this time still living in Baden-Baden, though she was to move to Berlin in the autumn of 1873, was continuing her extensive concertizing tours as one of the foremost pianists of Europe, specializing in the music of the classic tradition, by composers such as Schumann, Beethoven, Brahms, Schubert, Bach, Mendelssohn, Mozart, and Scarlatti. (She added the *Haydn Variations* to her repertoire in 1875.) Later (1878–92) she was on the faculty of the Hoch Conservatorium in Frankfurt/Main. She remained devoted to Brahms from the time of Robert's death (1856) to the end of her life; it is implicitly clear from the correspondence, however, that from

through the *Haydn Variations* for the first time. She apparently was not yet aware of the source of the theme or title of the work, for as she noted in her diary, ". . . In the morning I tried out with Johannes [his] new variations for two claviers on the ?-theme, which are entirely wonderful. . . ."[11]

Evidently, Clara had already informed Fritz Simrock (1837–1901), Brahms's publisher, that he had finished a new set of variations, two string quartets, and some songs, something which Brahms had neglected to mention to him. Simrock knew that Clara and her daughters were returning to Baden-Baden immediately, to be joined by Brahms for a few days of private music readings of his summer's production. The eager publisher then tried to persuade Brahms to let him travel along from Bonn to Baden-Baden to hear the new works. Brahms must have led Simrock to expect to meet him on the 9:00 A.M. train in Bonn on the 21st, but alas Brahms missed both the train and Simrock, who thereupon wrote a hasty letter to him in Tutzing asking what had happened and begging for some word about the new works. A second anxious letter was dispatched ten days later. By this time Brahms had returned (on the 27th) to Tutzing to continue his work. A week later he responded:

> I did not write you about the variations for two reasons. In the first place, I thought of Rieter [-Biedermann, his other publisher], and in the second place, they are actually variations for orchestra. More about it shortly, when I have made up my mind.[12]

Simrock's astonished rejoinder came from Ostende:

---

the late 1860s Brahms grew progressively less responsive to her advice and opinions with respect to his compositions.

11. ". . . Am morgen probirte ich mit Johannes neue Variationen für zwei Klaviere über das ?=Thema die ganz wundervoll sind. Das machte mir zum Beschluss auch grosse Freude." (Berthold Litzmann, *Clara Schumann, Ein Künstlerleben nach Tagebüchern und Briefen,* 3 vols. [Leipzig, 1902, 1905, 1908], III, p. 296.) Translation by the editor. The Grace E. Hadow translation of the Litzmann (*Clara Schumann, An Artist's Life,* 2 vols. [London, 1913; repr. New York, 1972], II, p. 299) inexplicably renders this as follows: "On the next day I tried over with Johannes the new variations on a theme of Haydn's, for two pianos. They are quite wonderful, and were a most happy ending to the Festival."

12. Letter (Sept. [4,] 1873), *Johannes Brahms Briefwechsel,* IX, p. 147; translation by the editor. Whether Brahms really considered publishing the work with Rieter-Biedermann or was merely teasing his friend Simrock (which he was frequently prone to do) is not known. Nothing in the collected correspondence with Rieter-Biedermann (*Johannes Brahms Briefwechsel,* XIV) suggests that he may have approached him about the *Haydn Variations.*

> The variations for orchestra? So much the better—[in French:] *that won't hinder the two pieces*—send them to me soon and do not think so much about Rieter but about the other "honest man" [pun on the name Biedermann]!! You probably have the score already finished and are having it played in Munich? I am very glad of it. . . .[13]

This revealing exchange of correspondence indicates for the first time in the Brahms literature that the *Haydn Variations* may have been intended for orchestra rather than for two pianos. One can find no evidence prior to this letter and a postcard to Levi on September 1st requesting a supply of orchestra manuscript paper[14] that Brahms had any other concept of the variations than as a work for two pianos. Therefore, it can merely be speculated that the trial reading with Clara Schumann may have suggested to him—as trial readings often brought about substantial revisions or even new concepts—that the work had symphonic potentiality and might be improved by orchestration. But more likely it may have occurred to him that the character of the work warranted two versions for different media, as had been the situation a few times previously (e.g., the *Sonata,* Op. 34*bis* for two pianos became the *Piano Quintet,* Op. 34).[15] At any rate, Brahms was able to complete the orchestration (which was already half finished when he ran out of paper and wrote to Levi) before he returned to Vienna around the middle of September.

The next project he had to deal with was to add finishing touches, including revisions, into the manuscript (already prepared by the Munich copyist) to serve as the engraver's layout score (*Stichvorlage*) for the two-piano version. He completed the job in due course and dispatched the score on October 4th to Fritz Simrock in Berlin. In his covering letter to Simrock, Brahms for the first time specified titles for the variations—

13. Letter (Sept. 6, 1873), *Johannes Brahms und Fritz Simrock; Weg einer Freundschaft. Briefe des Verlegers an den Komponisten,* ed. Kurt Stephenson (Hamburg, 1961), p. 64; translation by the editor.

14. Postcard [Sept. 1, 1873], *Johannes Brahms Briefwechsel,* VII, p. 137.

15. The other possible explanation would be that he had planned all along for an orchestral composition and wrote the two-piano version first only as a model for the ultimate version. The evidence however does not support this explanation. While the practice of writing a piano arrangement as a stage in the composition of large works was not unusual for Brahms, what is unusual here is the high degree of idiomatic technique in the two-piano version which stands on a par with that of the orchestral version which followed. None of the other pairs of versions share such equality. Brahms undoubtedly knew this to be the case, inasmuch as he subsequently insisted that the two were different versions of the same work, and gave them the numbers Op. 56a and Op. 56b to emphasize the equality. (However, he obviously was not decisive about this until after the first performance of the orchestral version.)

which hitherto had been called merely "Variations for Two Pianofortes" or "Variations for Orchestra"[16]—and indicated the honoraria he expected for the two versions. Moreover, he announced that the premiere of Op. 56a was being considered for the first Philharmonic concert, and that the success (or failure) of the performance could determine whether he would allow the orchestral version to be published:

> I am now allowing myself to be persuaded by extraordinary praise to send you the two-piano variations today. We intend to do them for orchestra in the first Philharmonic concert. But henceforth I should not like to know that the version for 2 pianos is being regarded as an arrangement and—have thought all sorts of things about it. Finally, I believe it might well be 2 titles:
>
> Variations for Orchestra on a Theme of Haydn, Op. 56a.
>
> Variations for 2 Pianofortes on a Theme of Haydn, Op. 56b.
>
> Afterwards a genuine arrangement for 4 hands could perhaps be expressly indicated underneath on both titles.
>
> As an honorarium I would then wish for each 500 *Reichstaler,* therefore 1000 [in all]. If I do not publish the orchestral variations, then it will be just 500 *Taler* and simply Op. 56.
>
> We will know by the beginning of November, and until then [they] can be so nicely engraved separately.
>
> It would, however, be at your own risk to some extent—in case I should perhaps change [something] after this performance! If you are worried about it, then postpone having the engraving done until then. To be sure, I do not believe it is urgent. But I am very confused with respect to these variations—wait and see what is to be done in the matter; even to send [them] back [to me] and to want to have nothing to do with all the fretting is right sensible.[17]

The fortuitous opportunity of a performance with the great Philharmonic (the Court Opera Orchestra) was initiated sometime prior to the end of September by *Kapellmeister* Dessoff, who begged Brahms for the premiere in the opening subscription concert of the season, and invited him to conduct it. This marked an important milestone in Brahms's growing recognition in Vienna, for only once before (1863) had one of his works been played by the Philharmonic, and that performance had been a disappointment.[18] During the month of October, the orchestral

16. Why he omitted any reference to the "Theme of Haydn" until this moment is not known. The autograph scores confirm that the titles were revised to their final form after the copying was finished (see page 153).

17. Letter (Sept. 1873; postmarked Oct. 4), *Johannes Brahms Briefwechsel,* IX, pp. 149–50; translation by the editor.

18. The first Vienna performance of the *Serenade,* Op. 16, for small orchestra (without violins), conducted by Dessoff, March 8, 1863. The orchestra was unenthusiastic about the work and some mishaps occurred during the performance.

parts were prepared by a copyist and Brahms made corrections and some revisions. The final rehearsal was scheduled for October 31st, in preparation for the concert on November 2nd. Brahms sent invitations for the rehearsal to several friends, among them Claus Groth, who was so impressed that he later wrote a recollection of the event in his memoirs:

> We were nearly alone in the great, magnificent hall . . . The A-major Symphony of Beethoven was being played in the meantime; I was delighted at the sonority of the splendid orchestra, to which I was completely unaccustomed. Brahms meanwhile was pacing back and forth or into an adjoining room and apologizing to me, which was not necessary, with the remark, "*Du,* I know this [piece] well enough!" Then the variations began. After a portion had been played, the conductor [Dessoff] stepped back from the podium, Brahms took off his overcoat—which gave me the impression that it was going to be an enormous muscular labor—mounted the podium, called out in his hoarse voice a word to the orchestra, who greeted him with a loud fanfare; then he commanded from memory the repetition of some passages—I was astonished [at] how he, without looking up, for example, called "Letter C . . ." and more of the same. I was enchanted and overcome by the glorious music. Billroth could not stay to the end [and] took his leave of me with the remark: "Tell Brahms I have had to be off; the composition has pleased me even in the particulars." This I naturally reported to Brahms at the conclusion with the addition: "That is also my opinion"; whereupon he replied to me in his ironically cheerful way (as he characteristically put it): "*Ja,* indeed, you are also unmusical!"[19]

The first performance took place in the Great Hall of the Gesellschaft der Musikfreunde, with Brahms conducting. The *Haydn Variations* was placed second on the program of this, the opening concert of the 1873–74 subscription series of Philharmonic Concerts. Otto Dessoff conducted a symphony ("Nr. 5, D-dur"—perhaps the *"Haffner" Serenade,* K. 250) by Mozart, the Overture to Schubert's opera *Alfonso und Estrella,* and *Symphony No. 7* by Beethoven.

The new work caused a sensation and received an enthusiastic review by Hanslick in *Die Neue freie Presse.*[20] Billroth wrote Brahms two days after the concert to express his enthusiasm for what he had heard (as well as for the new string quartets which had been dedicated to him):

> I had to be off the day before yesterday immediately after [the] conclusion of the rehearsal of your variations, to teach my boys to throw javelins and to revere the gods—so I could not say more to you [about] how beautiful I find your new work; it was worth very much to me today [in the concert] to greet it as an already good friend.—By no means do I want

19. Quoted by Kalbeck, *op. cit.,* II/2, pp. 478–79; translation by the editor.
20. The review, in translation, is included in the present edition on pages 211–13.

to speak about the artistic charm of the details, but only tell you what a pleasing impression the totality has made on me; the whole thing is so harmonically in sympathy with my disposition that, if I were at all able to write out a full score, I could write down the greatest portion of the work. The climax at the end is powerful! Goethe's words suddenly burst upon me: ". . . already he is outgrowing us in [his] mighty limbs—!" etc. —I hope you will keep your promise to send word to me immediately when your quartets are playable. So far as I have been able to observe from the scores, both quartets, like the orchestral variations, are conceived and worked out in the happiest mood; these pieces seem to me entirely out of the ordinary as beautiful, ripe, noble fruits; the concise forms greatly facilitate comprehension! I already owe you so much of the most beautiful hours of my inner life! Take my gratitude, as it comes from the heart.[21]

For his part Brahms was elated and so well satisfied with the worthiness of the orchestral version that he decided to let Simrock publish it; accordingly on the 7th he had Nottebohm carry the score with him on the train to Berlin.

Almost immediately a request came from the Bavarian Court *Kapellmeister* Wüllner for permission to give the second performance in Munich on December 10. Brahms agreed, but to make the performance possible, some expedients were required because the autograph score was already in the hands of the engraver Röder in Leipzig, the orchestra parts belonged to the Philharmonic in Vienna, and the Munich orchestra lacked the necessary contrabassoon. Brahms loaned Wüllner the fair-copy autograph of the two-piano version, Dessoff loaned the parts, and Brahms made a temporary modification in the orchestration.[22]

In lending the fair copy Brahms added a peculiar request, that after the concert the score should be sent to his friend Philipp Spitta.[23] This request may be considered yet another symbolic link between Brahms and his revered musical heritage, which he was able to realize in the

21. *Billroth im Briefwechsel mit Brahms, op. cit.*, pp. 44–45; translation by Margit L. McCorkle. Billroth's letter was dated November 4, but evidently was written on or shortly after November 2 because he must have been referring to the final rehearsal when he spoke of "the day before yesterday" (October 31) and of the concert when he spoke of "today." (In asking when the quartets would be "playable," he reminded Brahms that he awaited the four-hand piano arrangement (*Klavierauszug*) for a reading in his home.)

22. See pages 58–59.

23. Spitta was teaching at the Gymnasium in Sondershausen until 1874. The publication of volume one of his *J. S. Bach* in 1873 fully established his reputation as the leading Bach scholar. After the next year at the Nikolai Gymnasium in Leipzig, he was called as professor to the University of Berlin, where he became one of the founders of modern musicology.

Philharmonische Concerte.

Sonntag den 2. November 1873,

Mittags halb 1 Uhr, im

großen Saale der Gesellschaft der Musikfreunde:

1stes Abonnement-Concert

veranstaltet von den

Mitgliedern des k. k. Hof-Opern-Orchesters

unter der Leitung des k. k. Hof-Opern-Kapellmeisters Herrn

Otto Dessoff.

PROGRAMM:

Mozart . . . . . **Sinfonie** *Nr. 5, D-dur.*

Brahms . . . . **Variationen** *über ein Thema von Jos. Haydn (NEU)*
unter Leitung des Componisten.

Schubert . . . . **Ouverture** *zu „Alfonso und Estrella".*

Beethoven . . . **Sinfonie** *Nr. 7, A-dur.*

Streichinstrumente: Lemböck.

Das 2. Philharmonische Concert findet am 16. November 1873 statt.

Programme unentgeltlich.

Aus J. B. Wallishausser's k. k. Hoftheater-Druckerei. Z. n. st. G.

The program of the Philharmonic concert including the premier of the *Variations on a Theme of Haydn,* Vienna, November 2, 1873. (Courtesy Kurt Hofmann, Hamburg.)

Haydn Variations. Spitta and Brahms had maintained a mutual admiration since they first became acquainted in Göttingen around 1859, when Spitta was a philology student at the university. During the intervening years Brahms kept up an active interest in Spitta's researches on J. S. Bach and Buxtehude—as with Nottebohm's on Beethoven, Chrysander's on Handel, Pohl's on Haydn—and thus was understandably greatly moved when Spitta presented him with an advance copy of the first volume of his monumental Bach biography in May 1873. With the gift, Spitta wrote to Brahms,

> . . . there is no German whom I would rather the book might please than you. And as for what particularly concerns Sebastian Bach, I know altogether no one whose judgment of this master would be more important to me than yours.[24]

Brahms thereupon generously praised Spitta's efforts and thanked him most heartily for the gift.[25] Spitta next expressed his gratitude and confessed to a long-held, silent wish to possess a Brahms autograph. This was granted almost immediately, with a gift of the fair-copy autograph of the fugue from the *Chorale Prelude and Fugue on "O Traurigkeit, o Herzeleid."* Then, months later, on December 21st Spitta received the autograph of Op. 56b, as a surprise Christmas present.

A few days later Brahms himself was the recipient of a most remarkable Christmas present, which came as the unexpected culmination of this unusually eventful and fruitful year. Who could have imagined that Brahms and Wagner would be knighted simultaneously—fortuitously, *in absentia*—by King Ludwig II with the Bavarian Order of Maximilian II for highest distinction in the service of art and science! *Ritter von* Wagner was about to achieve his *Götterdämmerung,* and *Ritter von* Brahms was well on the way to his *First Symphony.*

24. Letter (May 14, 1873), *Johannes Brahms Briefwechsel,* XVI, p. 46; translation by the editor.

25. Letters (June [14], July 20/August 1, Dec. 29, 1873), *ibid.,* pp. 48–53.

Genesis and the Creative Process

Brahms was clearly not disposed to reveal to anyone the arcana of his composing workshop. Therefore, he destroyed virtually all evidence which could have been most revealing of the preparatory stage in his creative process—the laborious trial-and-error efforts associated with the genesis of his musical ideas and their elaboration up to the realization of a prototypal musical entity.[1] We do know, however, that for Brahms the invention of a composition usually began with a germinative idea which he characteristically derived from such inspirational stimuli as preexisting themes, personal experiences and events, Alpine scenery, Romantic literature, and the like. He himself described the phenomenon (in a later conversation with Sir George Henschel) as "simply an inspiration from above . . . [which] germinates unconsciously and in spite of ourselves."[2]

With respect to the *Haydn Variations,* we may never know for certain what stimulated him to compose the work, nor even when and how he was first inspired to do so. Max Kalbeck, nonetheless, speculated that the germ of a musical idea came to Brahms in the autumn of 1870 when his friend C. F. Pohl, then at work on his Haydn biography,[3] showed

1. For more details of Brahms's penchant for and success in keeping the secrets of his creative activity to himself, and for an extended discussion of the extant manuscripts as evidence of his creative process, see the editor's article (written in collaboration with Margit L. McCorkle) "Five Fundamental Obstacles in Brahms Source Research," in *Acta musicologica,* XLVIII/2 (1976).

2. See page 215.

3. *Joseph Haydn,* I (Leipzig, 1878). Pohl apparently completed the volume on July 25, 1875, the date of the foreword.

him a transcription which he (Pohl) had made of two pieces attributed to Haydn. One of these was the so-called *Chorale St. Antoni,* in open score for two oboes, two horns, three bassoons, and serpent. Brahms obviously was interested in both pieces—the other was the Andante from the *Symphony in B-flat Major* (Hob. I:16)—for he took the trouble to make his own transcripts for the loose-leaf collection of miscellaneous compositions he had been compiling since the 1850s.[4] Brahms copied the *Chorale St. Antoni* almost exactly as he saw it in Pohl's copy of the *Divertimento No. 1* attributed to Haydn (Hob. II:46), found by Pohl in the Gymnasium in Zittau (near Leipzig).[5]

Brahms naturally had no idea that the *Chorale St. Antoni* movement—or indeed all of the six divertimenti—would be regarded as spurious by Haydn scholars some eighty years after Pohl's discovery and his own attraction to the remarkably pregnant theme.[6] (Haydn research, it

4. They are together on one leaf (25.7 × 32.9 cm.) as obverse and reverse folios, contained in the loose-leaf folder identified as "Abschriften hervorragender Meisterstücke des 16.–18. Jahrhunderts zu Studienzwecken" (Vienna, Gesellschaft der Musikfreunde Archiv, A 130, Nos. 43 & 44). The date appended by Brahms to the symphony (obverse folio) led Kalbeck to remark (*Johannes Brahms,* 4 vols. in 8 [Berlin, 1908–14], II/2, p. 466), "How important the unexpected find was for Brahms, he himself confirmed, in that he placed the 'Novbr. 70' on his copy." The fact that the date may not pertain to the *Chorale St. Antoni* (reverse folio)—which from its appearance seems to have been copied at a different time, probably later—evidently did not concern Kalbeck. His unfounded assumption has been repeated ever since without question by most commentators and program annotators. In short, we have no proof that the theme was copied in or as early as November 1870.

It is significant, I think, that these two excerpts were the first to be added to his collection in perhaps a decade, when he had copied a Haydn Adagio to add to the existing representatives of the eighteenth century (fugal pieces and a chorale by Bach, a Handel Largo from a trio sonata, a chorus by Mattheson). These paled in comparison with the whole motets, Mass sections, chorales, and the like, selected from the previous two centuries. After the additions ca. 1870 no more items were copied for the collection.

5. Pohl's transcription of the *VI Divertimenti für Bläser* (Gesellschaft der Musikfreunde Archiv [VIII 41541]) contains the *Chorale St: Antoni* on leaves 3^v & 4^r of the so-titled *Divertimento I / à / 2 Oboi, 2 Klarinette* [sic], *2 Corni, 2 Fagotti obl. Fagotto / e Serpent / del Sign: / Giuseppe Haydn.* A comparison with Brahms's copy shows that Brahms made a few minor deletions and added, in the serpent staff, final cadence, an inexplicable penultimate eighth note on d (!) and an ultimate contra $B\flat_1$ for the Bassoon III (*"Fag*[*ott*]").

6. Since ca. 1951 the attribution of the *Chorale St. Antoni* theme to Haydn has been in serious doubt by one of the leading Haydn scholars, based on stylistic and circumstantial evidence. H. C. Robbins Landon has stated categorically that the six divertimenti are spurious. In the *Saturday Review of Literature* (August 25, 1951, p. 38) he suggested that "One of his [Haydn's] students, perhaps Pleyel, was probably the real author." Subsequently, in *The Musical Times* (July 1960, p. 433), "It is quite inconceivable that these six Divertimenti, either *in toto* or even in part, are by Joseph Haydn . . . The only correct approach, surely, is to say 'attributed to Haydn' . . . ."

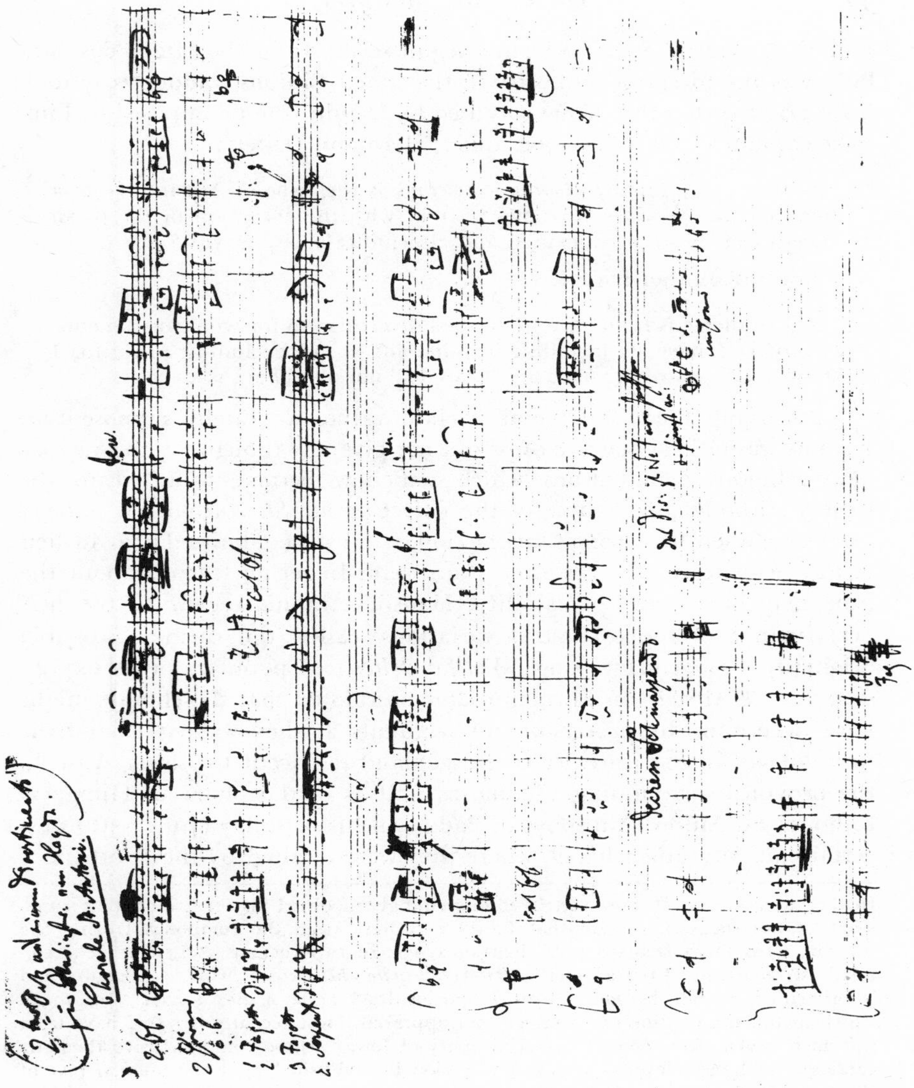

"Second movement from a divertimento for wind instruments by Haydn. *Chorale St: Antoni.*" Brahms's original transcript after a copy made by C. F. Pohl, the source for the theme for the *Variations on a Theme of Haydn*. Autograph manuscript, 1870(?), 25.7 × 32.9 cm. Gesellschaft der Musikfreunde, Vienna. Reproduced by permission.

should be remembered, had only begun seriously in the late 1860s, and Pohl was the foremost authority of the time.) Brahms undoubtedly took it for granted that the theme was used by Haydn if not composed by him, as he explained to his first biographer, Hermann Deiters:

> The theme for my *Haydn Variations* is the (whole) Andante from a divertimento for wind instruments. It is (with the exception of the [bass] strings) exactly so instrumented and also indicated by Haydn.[7]

And later to another friend:

> The theme is from an unpublished divertimento for wind instruments, exactly as I have it, including parallel fifths and excluding pizzicato. I know nothing further about the "Chorale," nor also about a text.[8]

Accepting these statements at face value, we might suppose that Brahms was either unaware of or did not give any thought to the various quasi-religious connotations which somehow became attached to the theme. Although the source of the title *Chorale St. Antoni* has not yet been explained to anyone's satisfaction, it must be admitted that in lieu of any evidence to the contrary, the several lingering legends about the tune may have some plausibility. Hanslick, in his review of the first performance of the orchestral variations, called the theme "probably originally a pilgrimage song (*Wallfahrtslied*) of popular, pious expression. . . ."[9] Alfred von Ehrmann later postulated that the chorale might have been sung by processions of penitents as they walked from their tiny villages in the province of Burgenland (adjacent to Lower Austria, the province surrounding Vienna, as well as to the plains of Hungary) to honor St. Anton (Anthony) of Padua on his feast-day (June 13th) at a certain St. Antonius Chapel, where they were awaited by the Brothers of

---

In the latter statement, however, Landon seemingly modified his former opinion somewhat by *not* suggesting again that Pleyel may have been the composer. During the interim, Otto Erich Deutsch published an article in two versions, "'Leider nicht von mir!' Musikalische Kuckuckseier" (*Österreichische Musikzeitschrift,* 11, 1956), and "'Unfortunately not by me' (Musical Spuriosities)" (*The Music Review,* 19, 1958), which included a citation of Landon's 1951 appraisal. Most recently (1975), I have been informed by Dr. Rita Benton (the University of Iowa), whose comprehensive thematic catalogue of Ignaz Pleyel (1757–1831) will soon be published, that the musical text of the so-called *Chorale St. Antoni* is *not* to be found among or within the compositions of this gifted, prolific pupil and sometime rival of Haydn.

7. From a letter to Deiters, September (really October), 1880. *Johannes Brahms Briefwechsel,* 16 vols. (Berlin, 1908–22; repr. Tutzing, 1974), III, p. 126. This excerpt and those that follow are translated by the editor, except where specifically noted.

8. From a letter to Julius Spengel, March 8, 1882. *Johannes Brahms an Julius Spengel. Unveröffentliche Briefe aus den Jahren 1882–1897,* ed. Annemari Spengel (Hamburg, 1959), p. 14.

9. See page 212 of this volume.

Mercy (*Barmherzigen Brüdern*).[10] The tune was supposedly already old when Haydn lived in Eisenstadt, now the capital of Burgenland, and thus would have been held in common currency as a folk song. Moreover, von Ehrmann suggested that the melody might have been used also in St. Anton's Day festivities at the Eisenstadt Palace park, as well as in *Feldpartiten* (divertimenti) to honor Prince Paul Anton Esterházy during the annual hunt on St. Anton's name-day.[11]

The furthest extreme in conjecture was the work of Brahms's biographer Kalbeck, who first met Brahms after the *Haydn Variations* appeared, and who published his darkly passionate program long after the composer's death.[12] Evidently confident that Brahms had indeed taken note of and been affected by the title *Chorale St. Antoni,* Kalbeck recorded another possible inspiration for the *Haydn Variations,* one related to the mystical significance of the Temptation of St. Anthony as a recurring theme in art. As it happened, Brahms and Kalbeck once had a conversation about the various pictorial representations of the St. Anthony legend with which the composer was familiar. Brahms, according to Kalbeck, felt that only one painter, Anselm Feuerbach, had "attempted to treat the story without magic contrivances, and his attempt was ill rewarded." In this comment he was obviously alluding to Feuerbach's work *The Temptation of St. Anthony* (1855), of which he possessed a daguerreotype reproduction made before the artist angrily destroyed the painting after its bad public reception. Brahms gave the photograph to Kalbeck with the enigmatic remark, "After all, the whole thing is no business for paintings. Poets and musicians could make a profit from it sooner."[13] Kalbeck must have believed that Brahms had let him in on the arcanum of creation, for he reported the conversation fully and based on it his own elaborately allegorical and analytical fantasy of the Brahms variations—not merely the *Chorale St. Antoni*—as a musical representation of the metaphysical interpretation of the St.

10. *Johannes Brahms; Weg, Werk und Welt* (Leipzig, 1933), p. 226.

11. *Ibid.*, p. 226. A similar opinion was evidently held by Geiringer when he prepared the first edition of the six *Feldpartiten* in 1932 and the English-language versions of his biographies, *Brahms* (Boston & New York, 1936) and *Haydn* (New York, 1946). But he did not go so far as to suggest which of the possible Princes Esterházy might have been thus honored. (The most likely candidates, perhaps, would have been either Prince Paul Anton I [1711–62] or Prince Paul Anton II [1738–94], or possibly even the ill-fated military-officer son of Paul Anton II, Anton [1767–90]. However, no evidence has been produced to support von Ehrmann's and Geiringer's linking of the *Chorale St. Antoni* or the "Haydn" divertimento with either Eisenstadt or the reigning Princes of Hungary.)

12. See pages 200–07 of this volume.

13. See page 203.

Anthony legend. It could be said, ironically, that in so doing, he leaned heavily upon the sort of "magic contrivances" which Brahms was pleased that Feuerbach had not needed. In the absence of more explicit information about how Brahms received his inspiration for this composition, it is interesting to speculate on the possible influence of the St. Anthony legend and particularly of the Feuerbach representation,[14] but we may doubt that Brahms actually conceived and organized his work to follow the musico-psychological course laid out by Kalbeck.

STAGES OF THE CREATIVE PROCESS

While we are unable to know how the *Haydn Variations* was conceived, invented, and elaborated prior to the substantially complete prototypal state shown in the earliest preserved drafts, we are on somewhat firmer ground when considering the creative process through analysis of internal elements in the finished work, and through textual comparison of the several manuscripts which show successive refinements and variants of the musical ideas. The former analytical effort has been approached differently, but with complementary results, in two penetrating studies by Leon Stein and Allen Forte (see pages 168 and 185). Although the focal points of their analyses are primarily the structural relationships of constituent components, nonetheless they have also contributed fine insights into the explicit and implicit possibilities of the preexisting theme, and the means by which Brahms perhaps realized these possibilities in composing his variations and finale. The latter analytical effort, that of textual comparison, was initially undertaken a half century ago by the Viennese musicologist and librarian Alfred Orel in a study of the sketches for the *Haydn Variations* following their first public exhibition (Gesellschaft der Musikfreunde, 1922). In his article[15] he presented some observations about Brahms's creative process, based on a comparison of the sketches with the archetypal fair-copy autograph and the first edition of Op. 56b, and included as illustrations his transcriptions of a few interesting sketches. Although his study was delimited more as an intro-

14. Two additional coincidences which may be peripherally related to the question of inspiration: Feuerbach's arrival in Vienna in 1873 to assume his professorship (which some biographers think was urged by Brahms) certainly caused the artist to be very much on the composer's mind (but not vice versa); and the etymological belief that the name "Brahms" derived from *Bram* (the broom shrub, whose blossom is known in Italy as the flower of St. Anthony), and thus the composer and the Saint had something in common, which no doubt tickled the composer's sense of humor.

15. "Skizzen zu Joh. Brahms' Haydn=Variationen," *Zeitschrift für Musikwissenschaft,* V/6 (March 1923), pp. 296–315.

duction to rather than a detailed analysis of the sketches, it continues to have some usefulness as a starting point for reviewing the unfolding progress of the whole composition.[16]

What follows, however, is a new survey of some especially notable features to be seen in the several manuscripts, showing visible evidence of progressive elaboration, refinement, and variation of prototypal ideas.

But first, it should be noted that we are more fortunate than Orel in now having a total of four manuscripts (as well as two corrected printed editions) for comparison. The manuscripts are the autograph sketches (*Skizzen*), the fair-copy autograph (*Reinschrift*) and the part-autograph (*Teilautograph*) of the two-piano variations, and the autograph score (*Partitur*) of the orchestral variations. (See pages 149–54 for a description of these manuscripts.) The part-autograph and the orchestral score were not available to Orel for his study because, having been used as engraver's layouts (*Stichvorlagen*) for the first editions, they remained the property of the N. Simrock firm until some years later.

The Sketches. It is most extraordinary that Brahms retained the sketches and permitted them to escape the fate of most of his preliminary sketches and drafts. After reconstructing and transcribing them for a clarified view of their contents, one can observe that the sketches represent three compositional levels (See Table 1 on pages 34–35 for a description of the manuscript, and pages 137–48 for the folios reproduced in facsimile): (1) full drafts for all variations, except V, and the finale, in varying degrees of completeness and usually clearly delineating the two piano parts; (2) rough drafts for portions of Variation V and the finale, containing only the most essential tonal and rhythmic material and usually condensing both piano parts into a single two-staff system; and (3) detail sketches for Variations I, II, V–VIII, and the finale, to work out problematic passages and note ideas for possible subsequent development. Included among these are a few short sketches of material not utilized in the work. The fact that the theme is omitted from the sketches is noteworthy, but presently inexplicable.

In all, within twelve folios (on six leaves), there are prototypes of

16. Two subsequent and rather superficial studies by the Beethoven scholar Paul Mies are "Aus Brahms' Werkstatt; Vom Entstehen und Werden der Werke bei Brahms," *N. Simrock Jahrbuch I,* ed. Erich H. Müller (Berlin, 1928), pp. 43–63, and "Der kritische Rat der Freunde und die Veröffentlichung der Werke bei Brahms," *N. Simrock Jahrbuch II* (Berlin, 1929), pp. 64–83. The former is more concerned with postulating the stages of Brahms's creative process generally through examination of the other extant sketches; the latter with describing through selected quotations from the correspondence the influence on various works of the criticisms of the composer's friends.

Table 1: Physical Description of the Sketches

Folio	*Staffs*	*Position*	*Contents*	*Remarks*
1	1–4, 8–11		Variation I: ink draft; pencil and ink revisions	
	5–7		Variation I: mm. 48 to end, sketch, ink and pencil, cancelled	
	12–15		Variation V: mm. 237–44, 257–59, rough sketch, pencil	Transcription, Ex. 5
	17–18	left third	Variation II: mm. 69–72, condensed sketch, pencil	Transcription, Ex. 1
2	1–14		Variation II: full draft, ink; pencilled revisions	
	15–18	left two-thirds	Unidentified pencil sketches of nine+ measures, discarded	
3	All		Variation III: full draft, ink; ink and pencil revisions	
4	1–4	to double bars	Variation VIII: mm. 322–31?, sketch, pencil	Transcription, Ex. 6
	5	left third		
4 (inverted)	1–9		Finale: rough draft of ostinato and Variants 1–6 and partial 7 (Brahms's nos. 2, 3, 4, 5, 6, 7, 8), pen and pencil	See Orel, pp. 302–04 Transcription of Variant 6, Ex. 14
	10–12	to double bar	Finale: Variant 7, pencil sketches	Transcription, Ex. 16
	13–14	center		
	14–18	to double bars	Finale: Variants 13/14, first sketch, pencil	Transcription, Ex. 18
5	All		Variation IV: full draft, ink; pencil and ink revisions	
6	1–14		Variation V: rough draft with detail sketches, ink and pencil	Transcription, Ex. 5
	15–16	center	Unidentified sketch, discarded	See Orel, p. 300
	15–16	right third	Variation VI: sketch, probably related to mm. 278–81, pencil	Transcription, Ex. 3
	17–18		Variation VI: mm. 264–279 + 1, rough sketch, pencil	Transcription, Ex. 2
7	1–4, 6–13		Variation VI: draft, ink and pencil; pencil and ink revisions	

8	1–4		Variation VII: draft through m. 304, ink; pencil and ink revisions	
	6	right third	Variation VIII: mm. 342–46, sketch, pencil	Transcription, Ex. 10
	6–9	left two-thirds	Variation VII: mm. 305–14, continuation of draft, pencil revisions	
	9	right third	Variation VIII: mm. 346–50, sketch, pencil	Transcription, Ex. 12
	11–12	right third	Variation VIII: mm. 342–46, discarded sketch, pencil	Transcription, Ex. 9
	12–15	to double bars	Variation VII: continuation from m. 314 to end, pencil	Transcription, Ex. 4
	14–15	after double bars	Variation VIII: mm. 350–54, sketch, pencil	Transcription, Ex. 13
	16–17	last 2 measures	Variation VIII: mm. 346–47, sketch, pencil	Transcription, Ex. 11
	16–18	left two-thirds	Variation VIII: mm. 332–41?, sketch, pencil	Transcription, Ex. 7
	18	last 4 measures	Variation VIII: mm. 342–45?, discarded sketch, pencil	Transcription, Ex. 8
9	1–15		Variation VIII: full draft, ink and pencil; pencilled revisions	
10	All		Finale: Variants 8 through 12 (ostinato entries 9–13), mm. 401–21, ink and pencil	
11	All		Finale: full draft from beginning through Variant 7 (ostinato entries 1–8), mm. 361–400, ink; pencil and ink revisions	Transcriptions of Variant 6, Ex. 15; Variant 7, Ex. 17
	8–9	right third	Finale: two partial-measure sketches for Variants 6 (m. 391) and 7 (m. 397)	Transcription, Ex. 20
12	1–4		Finale: full draft of Variants 15–16 (ostinato entries 16–17), mm. 436–45, pencil	
	6–9		Finale: full draft of Variants 13–14 (ostinato entries 14–15), mm. 426–35, pencil	Transcription, Ex. 19
	11–18		Finale: full draft of Coda, mm. 446–71, pencil	

the eight variations and the finale in more or less complete realization. Each is a clear—if in some instances only barely legible—approximation in abbreviated notation of the ultimate musical substance (melody, harmony, counterpoint, meter and rhythm, form) which constitutes the next stage, but with only slight indication of the expression devices and details of the more refined, archetypal fair copy. Orel was not far off the mark in suggesting that on the basis of the sketches alone it could be nearly possible to reconstruct the text of the two-piano version as we know it.[17]

From the physical appearance of the sketches we may surmise that the ease or difficulty Brahms experienced in elaborating the variations was in proportion to their degree of derivation from the theme and the complexity of chosen technical treatment. Each variation is identical to the theme in formal structure (except for one repeated measure in Variation IV), and is based on selected melodic, rhythmic, and harmonic nuclei from the theme; therefore, those which are most closely related to it and the simplest technically would generally pose the fewest problems for solution in preliminary sketches—i.e., I, II, III, IV, and to a slightly lesser degree VI and VII.

The first four variations are fluently and boldly notated in ink (folios 1, 2, 3, 5), suggesting that they evolved rather readily as contrapuntal embellishments, figurations, or elaborations of derived thematic ideas. Thus it would appear that no appreciable amount of sketching was required for working out the featured melodic motives and rhythmic patterns. The only exceptions are a cancelled sketch in the draft for the final eleven measures of Variation I; an almost illegible four-measure sketch on folio 1 for Variation II (Ex. 1); and an unidentified sketch, almost illegible and virtually unintelligible, of nine-plus measures on folio 2, which was perhaps an early idea for parts 2 and 3 of Variation II.

EXAMPLE 1: VARIATION II, MM. 69–72 (FOLIO 1)

17. Alfred Orel, "Skizzen zu Joh. Brahms' Haydn=Variationen," *Zeitschrift für Musikwissenschaft,* V/6 (March, 1923), p. 298.

Otherwise, only a few refinements of detail are pencilled into the essentially full drafts. These particular drafts are so complete, indeed, that one wonders whether they were not preceded by some subsequently destroyed preliminary sketches, which could explain their more finished state in comparison with those drafted variations following.[18] The fact that Variation IV, especially, was fully drafted with apparent ease is remarkable at the very least, when we recall that Tovey discerningly singled out the contrapuntal treatment of the two new melodies here as particularly exemplary:

> No one would guess that their combination is of an order of counterpoint which, at the beginning of the second strain, reaches to a development which the severest scholastic theorists have declared to be unattainable. It *is* unattainable by conscious calculation; but in great art these things happen, and the art is at no pains to conceal them—on the contrary, it owes its apparent simplicity to the fact that they are effective where less highly organized processes would be awkward.[19]

Variation VI was roughed out on folio 6 in a preliminary pencil sketch from the beginning through measure 279, with one extra measure of tentative continuation which was later discarded (Ex. 2). Superimposed above the final four measures of the sketch were two-plus measures which appear to be possible revisions and/or continuation (Ex. 3). A subsequent pen-and-pencil continuity draft on folio 7 shows only the principal ideas set out in the most abbreviated notation, apparently for completion later in the fair copy.

EXAMPLE 2: VARIATION VI, MM. 264–79 + 1, SKETCH (FOLIO 6)

18. While we have no evidence that the sketches and drafts were not entirely the product of the spring of 1873, my own presumption is that Brahms had perhaps done the preliminary sketching for Variations I–IV, at least, during the previous year. It is possible, of course, that Brahms himself may have removed and destroyed several leaves from the loose-leaf sketches, but there is no evidence to suggest that he did so.

19. Donald Francis Tovey, *Essays in Musical Analysis,* II: *Symphonies (II), Variations and Orchestral Polyphony* (London, 1935), p. 138.

EXAMPLE 3: VARIATION VI, MM. 278–81? (FOLIO 6)

The siciliano-like Variation VII, perhaps the least contrapuntally complex of the set, and seemingly functioning as a quasi-interlude, was fully drafted in ink on folio 8 to the beginning of the codetta (m. 314); following which, beneath, Brahms worked out in pencil sketch the final seven-and-one-half measures of the codetta, containing some subtle rhythmic counterpoint (Ex. 4).

In contrast to Variations I–IV and VI–VII, the highly chromatic, scherzo-like Variation V and the illusorily brief and most ingenious Variation VIII, caused the greater number of problems to be solved in sketches preliminary to and concurrent with the drafts, since these variations are much further removed from the theme and considerably more complex in concept, design, and virtuosity.

Variation V was laid out in this order: on folio 6, a rough pen-draft in condensed score through part 1 (mm. 206–25); a pencil sketch of part 2 (mm. 226–33), and a portion of part 3 with codetta (mm. 234–35, 240–42); a pen sketch in condensed score (mostly single staff) of the written-out repetition of parts 2 and 3 (mm. 245–58) as a skeletal representation of the principal material; and finally a pencil sketch in two systems of the concluding measures (260–63). In another leaf (folio 1), we find successively sketched the codetta (mm. 237–44) and the beginning of its

EXAMPLE 4: VARIATION VII, MM. 314–21 (FOLIO 8)

* Appoggiaturas not clear in the manuscript. They almost appear as doubled. 
† Only the dot is clear here; other notes may be in the manuscript.
‡ Top notes (small in the manuscript) seem to be as I have interpreted them here.
§ There seems to be another note or two (cancelled) in the treble/alto.

EXAMPLE 5: VARIATION V, COMPLETE (FOLIOS 1 AND 6)

* Top notes in this measure are not entirely clear in the MS.
† "Just return [repeat] from here."

‡ Another note or two may be here in the MS (illegible).

[?]
[254]
p
[Fol. 1]
[Fol. 6]
NB?

repetition (mm. 257–59) which ultimately were combined with the folio 6 sketch in the fair-copy autograph for the complete reading. Measure 236, not included in the sketches and draft, first appears in the fair copy. Example 5 (pp. 40–43) is a reconstructed transcription of the draft and sketches for Variation V.

Variation VIII was probably the most demanding of the set, though this fact is obscured by the fairly fluent appearance of the full draft on folio 9. Actually, the draft was preceded by eight partial (pencil) sketches on two previous leaves, in probably the following sequence:

> 1. Two rough sketches for part 1, the one on folio 4 most resembling the first two phrases, the other on folio 8 most relating to the repetition. However, it is apparent that Brahms did not fully utilize each in its discrete form, but instead exchanged and intermixed the ideas to constitute the thematic material for all of part 1 (Exx. 6 and 7). The one idea not included in the full draft of part 1 was that located on the top staff (mm. 2–5 in Ex. 7); the chromatic scale was subsequently incorporated within part 2 (m. 349, Pf. I) and the remaining three measures were discarded.

EXAMPLE 6: VARIATION VIII, MM. 322–31? (FOLIO 4)

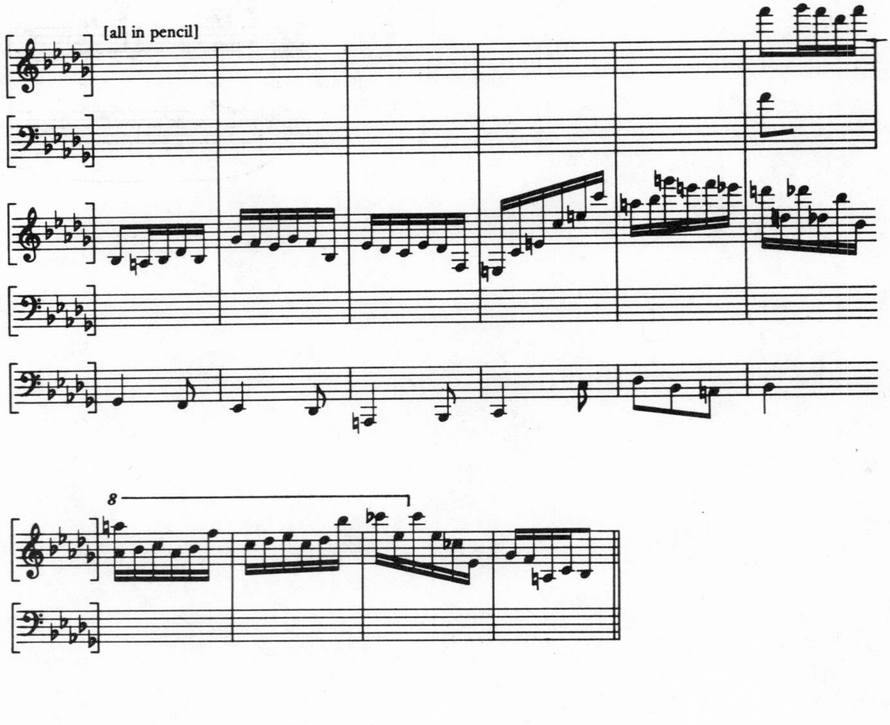

Example 7: Variation VIII, mm. 332–41? (folio 8)

* The lower notes are almost illegible, but seem to be as I have indicated them.

2. A discarded sketch on folio 8, partly illegible, might have been at first intended for part 2, phrase 1, which evidently would have had the section begin in the dominant minor (F minor) instead of the present dominant major (Ex. 8).

Example 8: Variation VIII, mm. 342–45?, discarded sketch (folio 8)

3. Two sketches on folio 8 for part 2, phrase 1. One was subsequently discarded (Ex. 9), and the other (Ex. 10) was transferred to the full draft but transposed to the lower octave.

EXAMPLE 9: VARIATION VIII, MM. 342–46, DISCARDED (FOLIO 8)

EXAMPLE 10: VARIATION VIII, MM. 342–46 (FOLIO 8)

4. Two sketches on folio 8 for part 2, phrase 2 (Exx. 11 and 12).

EXAMPLE 11: VARIATION VIII, MM. 346–47 (FOLIO 8)

EXAMPLE 12: VARIATION VIII, MM. 346–50 (FOLIO 8)

5. One sketch on folio 8 for the elision of part 2 and all of part 3, the outer voices of which were transferred to the full draft, though the bottom voice was transposed to the higher octave. While most of the material of the inner voices was subsequently discarded, the second attempt to introduce a chromatic scale, this time inverted (first measure of the sketch), is noteworthy (Ex. 13).

After working out these rudimentary details, Brahms drafted Variation VIII mostly in ink up to measure 353, but changed entirely to pencil for drafting the final eight measures, including the codetta, which he had not previously sketched. The two piano parts, however, were sketched

EXAMPLE 13: VARIATION VIII, MM. 350–54 (FOLIO 8)

* Virtually illegible notes in these two measures, tenor line; they appear to be as transcribed.

from measure 342 to the end with the Piano II material placed above that of Piano I, but Brahms subsequently switched them by pencilled Roman numerals in order to achieve equitable distribution. Moreover, all sketches and the pen-draft were notated in rhythmic units for $\frac{3}{8}$ meter! Evidently, after completing the draft, Brahms had second thoughts about the metric implications and thereupon asked himself most emphatically —with question marks—whether it should not be changed to $\frac{3}{4}$, which he then decided to do before preparing the fair copy.

And so having skillfully treated the thematic elements through some 466 measures (including all repeats) of sectional variations consisting of extraordinarily ingenious and felicitously expressive contrapuntal writing, Brahms was inspired to culminate the work with yet another set of variations, continuous variations now, in the style of a Baroque passacaglia. He chose for the basso ostinato a five-measure harmonic motive derived from the first phrase of the theme. From this motive, and together with it, he crafted sixteen variations and a coda, which in cumulative intensity and brilliant contrapuntal invention not only crown the variations but also apotheosize the *Chorale St. Antoni* theme. How did he construct this magnificent finale of 110 measures, effectively one-fifth of the whole composition? The drafts and sketches for the finale take up nearly all of four folios, as follows:

1. On folio 4, a very rough preliminary pen-and-pencil draft in condensed score with some figured-bass numerals, of the ostinato and variants 1 to 7, and pencil sketches for variants 7, 13, 14. After transferring the material to subsequent folios, Brahms drew a line across the entire sheet.

2. On folio 11, a full pen draft of the ostinato and variants 1 to 7, followed by a revision for variant 7, and finally (on leftover space on staffs 8 and 9), pencil sketches for two half measures of variants 6 and 7 to show rhythmic simplifications for a thinner texture, which were later incorporated within the fair copy.

3. On folio 10 (Brahms went back and used the blank folio opposite folio 11, so that the sequence of folios does not reflect the order in which he sketched), more or less full drafts of variants 8–11 in ink and variant 12 in pencil. Of these, variants 8, 10, and 11 are in two systems; variant 9 is condensed into a single system; and variant 12 lacks the ostinato.

4. On folio 12, the remainder of the finale in pencilled full draft. Here it is noteworthy that variants 15 and 16 are placed ahead of variants 13 and 14, after which follows the coda.

What conclusions may be drawn from these observations? Principally, that the gestation of the finale probably began around the time when Brahms was drafting Variation III, and the preliminary ideas were written down immediately in an extremely condensed, shorthand form as a memorandum. The drafting proper apparently occurred after completion of Variation VIII, and by and large the original ideas were developed with facility, with only a minimal amount of concurrent sketching required to work out a few of the more complicated textural problems. Certainly, also, the appearance of the finale serves to confirm a characteristic noted throughout the entire group of sketches, that nowhere is there to be seen any concept which was subsequently transformed into substantially different final form. Furthermore, by comparing the successive sketches and drafts in order to observe the evolution of variants 6, 7, 13, and 14—the only passages from the finale extant in several progressive stages—it can be seen that Brahms customarily refined his ideas through synthesis and simplification. The sketches and drafts of these four variants are given below in transcription (Exx. 14–20).

EXAMPLE 14: VARIANT 6, MM. 391–95, SKETCH (FOLIO 4)

[all in pencil except first three measures of ostinato]

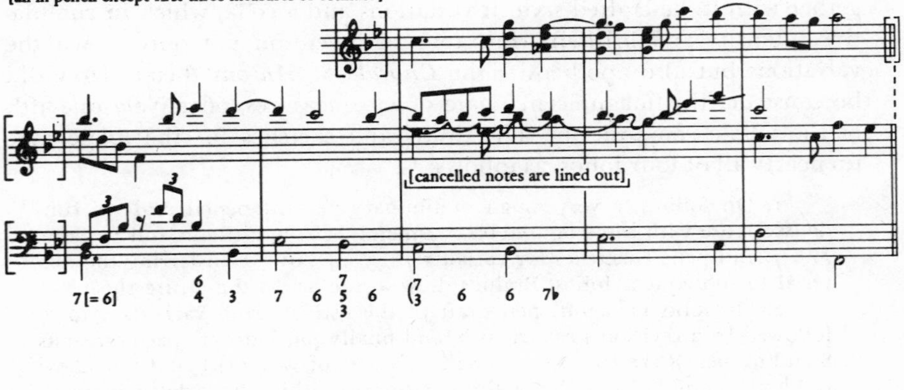

EXAMPLE 15: VARIANT 6, MM. 391–95, FIRST DRAFT (FOLIO 11)

Example 16: Variant 7, mm. 396–400, sketch 1 and revisions (folio 4)

EXAMPLE 17: VARIANT 7, MM. 396–400, DRAFT 1 AND REVISION (FOLIO 11)

EXAMPLE 17 (CONT'D)

EXAMPLE 18: VARIANTS 13/14, MM. 426–35+, SKETCH 1 (FOLIO 4)

* These notes in the treble appear to be what Brahms notated.

With respect to the general procedure of sketching and drafting, Brahms typically took short cuts to save time. In the sketches he more often than not omitted clefs, key and metric signatures, and used symbols for octave doubling (*8*), register changes (*8*¬), repetition of rhythmic patterns (*simile,* etc.), and repetition of figures, motives, and measures (·/.). In several instances his revised thinking about the assignment of Piano I and Piano II passages are indicated by transposition signs or boldly marked Roman numerals to exchange the parts in the pertinent places (in Variations II, III, V, VI, VIII, and finale). He used *N.B.* and large question marks abundantly to flag changes or problems for further consideration, such as whether to repeat the structural parts of Variations I and II, and which meter to settle on for Variation VIII. Also of some interest, and possible significance, is the fact that he used pen for the Roman numerals to indicate Variations I–III, but pencil for those for IV–VIII. The finale is not so labelled. It is interesting to attempt to determine whether he perhaps considered a different sequence for the latter variations. However, countless hours devoted to leaf rearrangement by innumerable combinations of possible foliation, and the examination of residual evidence of taped double leaves, dissimilar measurements of staffs and margins, incongruent folds, ash burns, and two soiled *verso* folios (revealing that at one time they were outer leaves) offer nothing but frustration. It is clear only that several different manuscript papers, none of them hallmarked or watermarked, were put together and that

EXAMPLE 19: VARIANTS 13 AND 14, MM. 426–35, FIRST DRAFT (FOLIO 12)

* Notes in alto line not clear; they might also be A–G–F–E.

EXAMPLE 20: VARIANT 6, M. 391, REVISION SKETCH, AND VARIANT 7, M. 397, REVISION SKETCH (FOLIO 11)

Brahms himself rearranged and inverted several leaves before they were foliated twice by the Gesellschaft der Musikfreunde archivists.[20]

The Elaboration Stages. Following this survey of the sketches, we need only consider briefly the archetypal stage (fair-copy autograph) and the final stage (part-autograph) of the creative process of Op. 56b. The first of these is a "fair copy" in that here Brahms copied the full drafts of the sketches, and in several instances finished or refined passages which had been left incomplete or in a somewhat rough state. The entire score is in ink and was copied fluently, from theme through finale, on manuscript paper similar to that used for the sketches. There are eighteen folios of music (on ten leaves) in all. The text is complete and both piano parts are now fully detailed, together with many more expression marks for articulation, phrasing, accents, and dynamics than were placed in the sketches. A few minor revisions and corrections of careless copying errors are easily noticed because of Brahms's custom of crossing out or obliterating with ink. Of most interest are the metric and tempo differences between the sketches and the fair copy with respect to Variation VIII. They show Brahms's concern that the variation might be performed too fast and vigorously as implicitly notated in the sketches. In the fair copy, he therefore changed the meter to $\frac{3}{4}$ from $\frac{3}{8}$, and the basic metric unit to eighth note from sixteenth. And then he moderated the tempo to *Poco presto* (from *Presto sempre mezza voce e legato*), but subsequently also struck out *Poco* and pencilled in *non troppo* to temper the remaining *Presto* (the *sempre m. v. e legato* was incorporated within the score).

20. Each leaf bears an "old" and "new" foliation, supplied by two archivists of the Gesellschaft der Musikfreunde, pencilled at the bottom (old) and top (new), and are equated as follows: (old) fol. 5 = (new) fol. 1, fol. 6 = fol. 2, fol. 7 = fol. 3, fol. 8 = fol. 4, fol. 9 = fol. 5, fol. 10 = fol. 6, fol. 11 = fol. 7, fol. 12 = fol. 8, fol. 13 = fol. 9, fol. 14 = fol. 10, fol. 15 = fol. 11, fol. 16 = fol. 12. The old foliation began at folio 5 to count the modern front cover and blank flyleaf.

The part-autograph was made from the fair copy, evidently to serve as a second copy for Brahms's trial reading with Clara Schumann after the Schumann Memorial Festival. A copyist prepared a score, but copied only the Pianoforte I part for the theme and variations, leaving space for the eventual addition of the Pianoforte II part, and a complete score of the finale. He filled in all formerly abbreviated passages with the exception of left-hand material for Pianoforte I in Variation III, mm. 89, 91–97. Brahms himself then supplied the second part (still using some abbreviations), changed a few details of expression and voicing, allowed the copyist's *Poco presto* in Variation VIII to stand (!), and in the finale added the optional *ossia* and replaced the original *Vivace* with *in tempo.* This manuscript thus became the most finished version and was used as the engraver's layout for the aborted original first edition, printed in late 1873.[21]

The Orchestral Transcription. We may surmise from the autograph score that Brahms's task in preparing an orchestral transcription was largely a matter of orchestrating the two-piano version and solving a few problematic details of sonority and balance. It is likely that he accomplished the work with but a slight amount of additional compositional effort. The result was a setting for full orchestra (including piccolo, contrabassoon, and triangle but without trombones), essentially in the orchestration styles of Beethoven and Schumann, in which the contrasting groups of strings and winds divide and alternately exchange the thematic and harmonic material throughout. He evidently decided it was unnecessary to make more than a few obligatory alterations in the melodic elements to accommodate the orchestral idiom and texture. On the other hand, he did make a number of significant modifications in articulation, phrasing, dynamics, and meters which were more idiomatic for the original two-piano version. The meter changes in the several stages of evolution, from sketches to the printed edition of the orchestral version, provide an interesting illustration of Brahms's concern for indicating his tempos with great care and clarity. The progressive refinement of his tempos can be shown by the comparison chart (Table 2, page 57).

The choice of appropriate instrumentation and combinations must have been a temporary problem in a few passages, as we may observe in the several important revisions in registration, placement, and doubling.

21. See page 152, n. 6.

Table 2

	Sketches	Autograph (Op. 56b)	Part-Autograph and Printed Score (Op. 56b)	Autograph (Op. 56a)	Printed Score (Op. 56a)
Theme	[None]	*Andante*	*Andante*	*Andante*	*Andante*
Var. I	*Andante con moto*	*Andante con moto*	*Andante con moto*	[No indication]	*Poco più animato*
Var. II	*Vivace*	*Vivace*	*Vivace*	~~*Vivace*~~ *Più vivace*	*Più vivace*
Var. III	*con Moto*	*con Moto*	*Con moto*	*con moto*	*Con moto*
Var. IV	*Andante* ~~*con moto*~~ *dol. e sempl.*	*Andante*	*Andante*	*Andante con moto*	*Andante con moto*
Var. V	*Presto*	*Presto*	*Presto*	~~*Vivace*~~ *poco Vivace*	*Vivace*
Var. VI	*Vivace*	*Vivace*	*Vivace*	*Vivace*	*Vivace*
Var. VII	*Grazioso*	*Grazioso*	*Grazioso*	*Grazioso*	*Grazioso*
Var. VIII	*Presto* ~~*ma poco e espress*~~*. sempre m. v. e legato*	~~*Poco*~~ *presto non troppo*	*Poco presto*	*Presto non troppo*	*Presto non troppo*
Finale	*Andante*	*Andante*	*Andante*	*Andante*	*Andante*

Examples are in Variation V, where the double basses initially had been placed in unison with the cellos (mm. 207–11, 229–32, 248–51) and the flute was first in unison with the piccolo and clarinet solos (mm. 229–32); and in Variation VII where the first violins previously played both first and second parts (*divisi*) while the second violins played an octave lower than in the final version (mm. 293–96). Coincidentally, the delightful double appoggiatura, with which Variation VII begins in Op. 56b, was initially assigned to flute, first violins, and violas, but then cancelled altogether. Also in this variation, Brahms once again faced the problem of how to achieve the desired subtlety in the rhythmic counterpoint in the first four measures of the codetta (mm. 315–18). His first solution was to have the violas continue (from mm. 311–15) the dotted rhythmic pattern (doubling the clarinet) in mm. 315–18, the second violins taking a turn with it (doubling the flute) in mm. 316–17, and finally the first violins (also doubling the flute) concluding the motive in mm. 317–18. Since the effect of this doubling would have been to emphasize the one motive over the other two simultaneous counterrhythmic patterns, he therefore eliminated the doubling in order to balance the rhythmic counterpoint, thus intensifying its subtlety.

By far the most important revision was the last-minute elimination, before the Vienna premiere, of a serious miscalculation which would have significantly altered the balance and character of the entire work. Evidently it had been Brahms's idea originally to assign to the violins and violas the major responsibility in the theme—doubled by oboes and bassoons—which would have effectively negated the distinctive wind-band sonority of the *Chorale St. Antoni* as he had discovered it. Apparently sensing this, he crossed out the string parts and kept the more rustic setting, recognized ever since as an inspired feature of his masterly conception.

Another potential mistake—that of substituting some other low bass wind for the contrabassoon—was averted after much pondering. The question arose during the preparations for the Munich concert, because the Opera Orchestra lacked a contrabassoon—in its old form, it was by now obsolete and rare. In the meantime, he exchanged correspondence with the two conductors, Wüllner and Levi, about the advisability of substituting either a bass trombone or tuba. To Wüllner (who was preparing to conduct the performance) he prescribed the *trombone,* but with reservations,[22] and shortly afterwards he told Levi (who was disap-

22. Letter (November 1873), *Johannes Brahms Briefwechsel,* XV, p. 49.

pointed not to be conducting) that he had asked Wüllner whether it might not be better to leave out the *tuba!*[23] Thereupon he wrote to Fritz Simrock to inquire if the tuba part was in order.[24] Indeed, he even went so far as to add a footnote to the autograph score, stating, "The contrabassoon can be replaced if necessary by a tuba (however only in the theme and in the finale), utilizing the accompanying [separate] part."[25] By the middle of December he was so troubled by the thought of the tuba that he wrote urgently to Simrock, requesting the substitution of a third bassoon as the alternate instrument.[26] A week later he (fortunately) begged Simrock to forget the whole business,[27] and so the original conception and the contrabassoon part remained inviolate.

In the resolution of all this indecision Brahms staked the future of the ideally balanced *Haydn Variations* for orchestra upon the unknown rather than the unthinkable: that is, with no foreknowledge that the currently unsatisfactory contrabassoon would become a standard instrument after its reconstruction by Heckel in 1879, and probably with certain knowledge that a bass tuba part would more likely than not be played on the recently invented *Wagner-Tube,* instead of its less obtrusive predecessors and more obtrusive successors.[28]

23. Letter (November 1873), *Johannes Brahms Briefwechsel,* VII, p. 147.

24. Letter (November 1873 [postmarked December 6]), *Johannes Brahms Briefwechsel,* IX, pp. 158–59.

25. "Das Contrafagott ist nöthingenfalls (jedoch nur im Thema und im Finale) nach beiliegender Stimme durch eine Tuba zu ersetzen." It is important to observe that this note was added several weeks after the first performance, and there is no support for Kalbeck's assertion (*op. cit.,* II/2, p. 479) that Brahms first considered the use of the tuba during the rehearsals for the Vienna premiere.

26. Letter (December 14, 1873), *Johannes Brahms Briefwechsel,* IX, p. 162.

27. Letter (December 20, 1873), *ibid.,* p. 163.

28. However, his preference for the contrabassoon as opposed to the tuba was not altogether permanently settled. It is a point of some interest that he stayed with the contrabassoon—which form is not known—rather than the tuba for his *First Symphony* (ca. 1874/1876), but chose the tuba instead for the *Second Symphony* (1877). For the *Third Symphony* (1883) and the *Fourth* (1884/1885) he settled again on the contrabassoon, by that time quite a different sounding instrument than the traditional versions he had known earlier. (Some sense of this situation is given in Lyndesay G. Langwill, *The Bassoon and Contrabassoon* [London & New York, 1965], pp. 118 f.)

THE SCORE OF THE VARIATIONS FOR ORCHESTRA

Edited by
HANS GÁL

Revised by
DONALD M. McCORKLE

ACKNOWLEDGEMENT

The two scores reprinted here are substantially the original *Johannes Brahms Sämtliche Werke* editions of the Gesellschaft der Musikfreunde, Vienna (editors: Hans Gál [1926] and Eusebius Mandyczewski [1927], Leipzig, Breitkopf & Härtel, 1926–28). The revisions incorporated by this editor were made expressly for this Norton Critical Score edition and are detailed in the Textual Criticism and Notes, beginning on page 149.

INSTRUMENTATION

Piccolo (*Kleine Flöte*)
2 Flutes (*Flöten*)
2 Oboes (*Oboen*)
2 Clarinets in B♭ (*Klarinetten in B*)
2 Bassoons (*Fagotte*)
Contrabassoon (*Kontrafagott*)
4 Horns (*Hörner*)
  2 in B♭ (*in tief B*)
  2 in E♭ (*in Es*)
2 Trumpets in B♭ (*Trompeten in B*)
Timpani in F, B♭ (*Pauken in F, B*)
Triangle (*Triangel*)
Violin I (*1. Violine*)
Violin II (*2. Violine*)
Viola (*Bratsche*)
Violoncello (*Violoncell*)
Double Bass (*Kontrabass*)

VARIATIONS ON A THEME OF HAYDN FOR ORCHESTRA

Chorale St. Antoni

11
Fl.
Ob.
Klar. (B)
Fag.
K.-Fag.
(B) Hr. (Es)
Trpt. (B)
1. Viol.
2. Viol.
Br.
Vcl.
K.-B.
p
pp
f
mf
21
a 2
ten.
dim. smorz.
1.
2.

30
Var. I
Poco più animato
Kl. Fl.
Fl.
Ob.
Fag.
K.-Fag.
(B) Hr. (Es)
Pk.
1. Viol.
2. Viol.
Br.
Vcl.
K.-B.
a 2
arco
Poco più animato
40
Klar (B)
Trpt. (B)
ten.
cresc.

49
Kl.Fl.
Fl.
Ob.
Klar. (B)
Fag.
K-Fag.
(B) Hr. (Es)
Trpt. (B)
Pk.
1.Viol.
2.Viol.
Br.
Vcl.
K.-B.
a 2
dim.
p
f

Var. II
Più vivace
59
Kl.Fl.
Fl.
Ob.
Klar. (B)
Fag.
K.-Fag.
(B)
Hr.
(Es)
Trpt. (B)
Pk.
1.Viol.
2.Viol.
Br.
Vcl.
K.-B.
pizz.
arco
Più vivace

69
Kl. Fl.
Fl.
Ob.
Klar. (B)
Fag.
K-Fag.
(B) Hr. (Es)
Trpt. (B)
Pk.
1. Viol.
2. Viol.
Br.
Vcl.
K.-B.
div.
arco
pizz.
tr

79
Kl.Fl.
Fl.
Ob.
Klar. (B)
Fag.
K.-Fag.
(B)
Hr.
(Es)
Trpt. (B)
Pk.
1.Viol.
2.Viol.
Br.
Vcl.
K.-B.
f
dim.
p
sf
tr
più f
arco

Var. III
Con moto
88
Fl.
Ob.
Klar (B)
Fag.
Hr. (B)
1.Viol.
2.Viol.
Br.
Vcl
K.-B.
p dolce e legato
p dolce e legato
p
1.
p dolce
pp legato
pp
Con moto
A
98
Fl
Ob.
Klar. (B)
Fag.
Hr. (B)
1.Viol.
2.Viol.
Br.
Vcl.
K. B.
p molto dolce
p molto dolce
legato
p dolce legato
pp
A

105
B
Fl.
Ob.
Klar. (B)
Fag.
1.2.
(B)
Hr.
(F)
in F
1.Viol.
2.Viol.
Br.
Vcl.
K.-B.
dolce
114
B
Hr. (F)
in Es
(Es)
pp

125
C
Fl.
Ob.
Klar. (B)
Fag.
(B) Hr. (F)
1.Viol.
2.Viol.
Br.
Vcl.
K.-B.
p
132
p molto dolce
p molto

139
Fl.
Ob.
Klar. (B)
Fag.
(B) Hr. (F)
1.2.
3.
2.
1.Viol.
2Viol.
Br.
Vcl.
K.-B.
p
rit.
dim.
Var. IV
146
Andante con moto
1.
p dolce e semplice
più f
2.Viol.
p dolce
pizz.
arco
Andante con moto

D
156
Fl.
Ob.
Klar. (B)
Fag.
1.Viol.
2.Viol.
Br.
Vcl.
K.-B.
p dolce e semplice
pizz.
arco
più f
mf
D
166
E
Hr. (B)
E

176
Fl.
Ob.
Klar. (B)
Fag.
Hr. (B)
1.Viol.
2.Viol.
Br.
Vcl.
K.-B.
1. 2.
1.
p
sf
p semplice
F
186
più f
pizz.

196
Fl.
Ob.
Klar. (B)
Fag.
1. Viol.
2. Viol.
Br.
Vcl.
K.-B.
p semplice
arco

Var. V
206
Vivace
Kl. Fl.
Fl.
Ob.
Klar. (B)
Fag.
Hr. (B) (F)
1. Viol.
2. Viol.
Br.
Vcl.
K.-B.
sfp legg.
p legg.
pp legg.
Vivace

214
G
Kl.Fl.
Fl.
Ob.
Klar. (B)
Fag.
Hr. (B)
1.Viol.
2.Viol.
Br.
Vcl.
K.-B.
a 2
sfp
sf
f
1.2.
legg.
222
H
pp legg.
1.
3.
(F)
arco
p

230
Kl.Fl.
Fl.
Ob.
Klar. (B)
Fag.
Hr. (B)
1.Viol.
2.Viol.
Br.
Vcl.
K.-B.
pp legg.
p sempre
pp sempre
pizz.
238
I
Hr. (B)
Hr. (F)
arco

247
Kl.Fl.
Fl.
Ob.
Klar. (B)
Fag.
Hr. (B)
Hr. (F)
1.Viol.
2.Viol.
Br.
Vcl.
K.-B.
pp legg.
a 2
pizz.
255
pizz.

264
Var. VI
Vivace
Kl.Fl.
Fl.
Ob.
Klar. (B)
Fag.
K.-Fag.
(B)
Hr. (F)
(Es)
Trpt (B)
Pk.
1.Viol.
2.Viol.
Br.
Vcl.
K.-B.
a 2
1.
1. 2.
3.
4.
p sempre
pizz.
arco
Vivace

272
1.
2.
Kl.Fl.
Fl.
a 2
Ob.
Klar. (B)
Fag.
a 2
K.-Fag.
(B)
Hr. (F)
(Es)
Trpt. (B)
Pk.
1.Viol.
arco
2.Viol.
arco
Br.
Vcl.
K.-B.

278
Kl.Fl.
Fl.
Ob.
Klar. (B)
Fag.
K.-Fag.
(B)
Hr.(F)
Es)
Trpt. (B)
Pk.
1.Viol.
2.Viol.
Br.
Vcl.
K.-B.
a 2
sf
f
ff
marc.

286
Kl. Fl.
Fl.
Ob.
Klar. (B)
Fag.
K.-Fag.
(B)
Hr. (F)
(Es)
Trpt. (B)
Pk.
1. Viol.
2. Viol.
Br.
Vcl.
K.-B.
a 2

Var. VII
Grazioso
293
Fl.
Ob.
Klar. (B)
Fag.
Hr. (B)
1.Viol.
2.Viol.
Br.
Vcl.
K.-B.
p dolce
a 2
dolce
Solo
p espress.
p dolce
Grazioso
300
Hr. (F)
(Es)
legato

307
Fl.
Ob.
Klar. (B)
Fag.
Hr. (B) (F) (Es)
1. Viol.
2. Viol.
Br.
Vcl.
K.-B.
p dolce
dolce
p espress.
espress.
div.
315
cresc.
p dim.
pp
in Es

Var. VIII
322
Presto non troppo
Kl. Fl.
Fl.
Ob.
Klar. (B)
Fag.
1. Viol.
2. Viol.
Br.
Vcl.
con sord.
pp sempre
1.
Presto non troppo
330
K
K. Fag.
Hr. (B)
Pk.
1. 2.
pp
p
tr

339
Kl.Fl.
Fl.
Ob.
Klar. (B)
Fag.
(B) Hr. (Es)
Pk.
1.Viol.
2.Viol.
Br.
Vcl.
K.-B.
tr
1.
1°
3.
a 2
pp
p sempre
pizz.
arco
p
347
Kl.Fl.
Fl.
Ob.
Klar. (B)
Fag.
(B) Hr. (Es)
1.Viol.
2.Viol.
Br.
Vcl.
Vcl.
1.
a 2
p
pp
arco

354
Kl.Fl.
Fl.
Ob.
1.
Klar.
(B)
Fag.
K. Fag.
(B)
Hr.
(Es)
3.
Trpt
(B)
Pk.
1.Viol.
2.Viol.
Br.
Vcl.
K. B.
pp
pizz.
arco

Finale

361
Andante
Fl.
Ob.
Klar. (B)
Fag.
K.-Fag.
Hr. (B)
1. Viol.
2. Viol.
Br.
Vcl.
K.-B.
p leg.
senza sord.
div.
1. 2.
p
372
Andante
Pk.
unis
cresc.
a 2
f
L

381
Fl.
Ob.
Klar. (B)
Fag.
K.-Fag.
(B) Hr. (Es)
Trpt. (B)
Pk.
1. Viol.
2. Viol.
Br.
Vcl. K.-B.
390
M
a 2
ten.
più f
sf cresc.

398
Fl.
Ob.
Klar. (B)
Fag.
K.-Fag
(B) Hr. (Es)
Pk.
1. Viol.
2. Viol.
Br.
Vcl.
K.-B.
a 2
ff
f
dim.
p
tr
div.
p dolce
pizz.
404
N
1. Solo
1. 2.
pp legg.
pp
arco
N

409
Fl.
Ob.
Klar. (B)
Fag.
Hr. (B)
1.Viol.
2.Viol.
Br.
Vcl.
K.-B.
1.
1.2.
molto dolce
molto dolce
molto dolce
pp
pp
p
pizz.
414
Solo
1.
dolce
p semplice
1.
pizz.

419
Fl.
Ob.
Klar. (B)
Fag.
Hr. (B)
1.Viol.
2.Viol.
Br.
Vcl.
K.-B.
dolce
pizz.
424
O
Trpt. (B)
a 2
p ma marc.
cresc.
1. 2.
arco
p

431
Kl. Fl.
Fl.
Ob.
Klar. (B)
Fag.
K.-Fag.
(B) Hr. (Es)
Trpt. (B)
Pk.
1. Viol.
2. Viol.
Br.
Vcl.
K.-B.
a 2
p marc.
poco cresc.
cresc.
f marc.
poco f
p
mf
div.
poco più f cresc.
poco f cresc.

437
Kl. Fl.
Fl.
a 2
Ob.
f marc.
Klar. (B)
Fag.
K.-Fag.
(B) Hr. (Es)
Trpt. (B)
mf
Pk.
Trg.
p ben marc.
pp
cresc.
div.
1. Viol.
2. Viol.
Br.
Vcl.
K.-B.
p marc.
p

444
P
Kl. Fl.
Fl.
Ob.
Klar. (B)
Fag.
K.-Fag.
(B)
Hr.
(Es)
Trpt. (B)
Pk.
Trg.
1. Viol.
2. Viol.
Br.
Vcl.
K.-B.
a 2
f marc.
(ff)
ff ben marc.
ff marc.
P

450
Kl. Fl.
Fl.
Ob.
Klar. (B)
Fag.
K.-Fag.
(B)
Hr.
(Es)
Trpt. (B)
Pk.
Trg.
1. Viol.
2. Viol.
Br.
Vcl.
K. B.
a 2

455
Kl. Fl.
Fl.
Ob.
Klar. (B)
Fag.
K.-Fag.
(B) Hr. (Es)
Trpt. (B)
Pk.
Trg.
1. Viol.
2. Viol.
Br.
Vcl.
K.-B.
a 2
ff
sf
f
tr

460
rit.
Kl. Fl.
a 2
Fl.
dim.
p dim.
Ob.
Klar. (B)
Fag.
K.-Fag.
(B)
Hr.
(Es)
Trpt. (B)
pp dim.
Pk.
p
Trg.
1. Viol.
2. Viol.
Br.
Vcl.
K.-B.
6
rit.

465
molto rit.
in tempo
Kl. Fl.
Fl.
Ob.
Klar. (B)
Fag.
K.-Fag.
(B)
Hr.
(Es)
Trpt. (B)
Pk.
Trg.
1. Viol.
2. Viol.
Br.
Vcl.
K.-B.
pp
ff
f
dim.
tr
molto rit.
in tempo

The Score of the Variations for Two Pianos

Edited by
EUSEBIUS MANDYCZEWSKI

Revised by
DONALD M. McCORKLE

VARIATIONS ON A THEME OF HAYDN
FOR TWO PIANOS

23
I
II
dim. smorzando
p
f
1.
2.
8
Var. 1
30
Andante con moto
Andante con moto
p
3
35
mf

40
I
II
f
44
p
dim.
49

54
I
II
p
dim.
dim.
Var. 2
Vivace
59
f
p
Vivace
f
p
64
f
p
f
p

69
I
II
f
p
pp
75
f
p
più f
82
dim.
8

Var. 3
Con moto
88
p dolce e legato
p
I
Con moto
p legato
II
p
96
p sempre e legato
molto p dolce e legato
102
p
8

108
I
II
p
dolce
116
I
II
p
p
124
I
II
p

130
I
II
135
p
p dolce
140
rit. dim.
rit. dim.

Var. 4
Andante
146
dolce e semplice
p
I
Andante
p dolce
II
151
più f
I
più f
II
156
p
I
più f
p espress.
II
più f

162
I
II
p
168
174
poco f
p
sfz

180
sfz
semplice
I
p
sfz
II
p
sfz
186
I
p
II
p
192
I
poco f
p
poco f
II
p

199
I
II
sfz
p
p semplice
206
Var. 5
Poco presto
8
I
II
sfz
p
Poco presto
sfz p
211
I
II
f
p

216
221
226
I
II
sfz p
sfz
f
p

230
I
II
p
sfz
235
p legg.
legg.
p sempre
240

245
I
II
f
p
249
p sempre e legg.
254

259
I
p
II
p
264 Var. 6
Vivace
I
f
Vivace
II
p
f
269
I
p sempre
1.
2.
II
p sempre
1.
2.

274
I
II
f
sfz
278
marc.
283

288
I
II
sfz
f
sf
Var. 7
Grazioso
293
p
Grazioso
p molto dolce
298
molto dolce

303
I
II
p
legato
307
molto dolce
312
espress.

317
8
I
II
Var. 8
322
Poco presto
I
Poco presto
II
p sempre m. v. e legato
327
p sempre m. v. e legato
I
8
II

332
I
II
337
I
II
342
p
I
II

346
I
II
p
351
sempre molto p
non leg.
non leg.
sempre molto p
356
8
non leg.

361
Finale
Andante
p legato
I
Andante
p legato
II
367
I
II
373
I
cresc.
3
II
cresc.
3

378
I
II
f
383
8
sempre più f
sempre più f
387

391
I
II
più f
più f
394
sfz
cresc.
sfz
397
f
f

ossia
400
I
II
p
dolce
f
p dolce
403
406
p
p dolce

409
I
II
p dolce
sempre dolce e grazioso
412
I
II
415
I
II
p grazioso
p

418
I
II
421
molto dolce
425
marc.
p
m.s.
p

429
I
II
433
cresc.
più f
cresc.
poco più f ben marcato
437
p ma ben marc.

441
I
II
poco più animato sempre
p ma ben marcato
cresc.
cresc.
444
f marc. e sempre cresc.
f
447
ff
ff

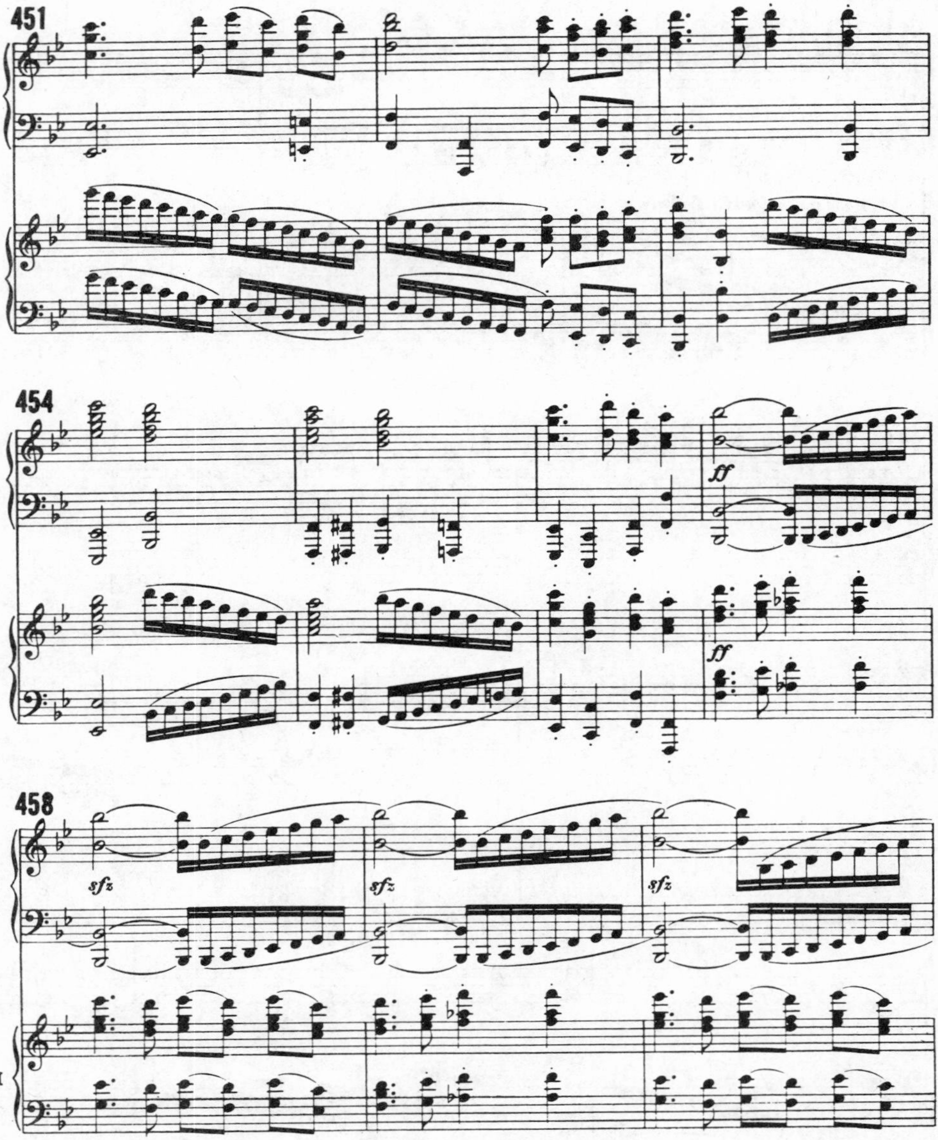
451
I
II
454
ff
ff
458
sfz
sfz
sfz

461
I
II
463
p dim. e ritard.
molto ritard. e dim.
I
p dim. e ritard.
molto ritard. e dim.
II
467
in tempo
ff
8
I
in tempo
ff
II

The Sketches

ACKNOWLEDGEMENT

Brahms's complete sketches are here printed in facsimile, photographically reproduced from the autograph manuscript in the possession of the Gesellschaft der Musikfreunde, Vienna (A118, Brahms *Nachlass*), and are published for the first time by permission of the Gesellschaft. The manuscript consists of 6 leaves (12 folios of music), 27 × 34 cm., 18 staffs on wove paper, without watermarks or hallmarks, and is bound in later boards. It is without title, signature, and date. The lighter notation was done in lead pencil, which in some instances is almost illegible in the manuscript.

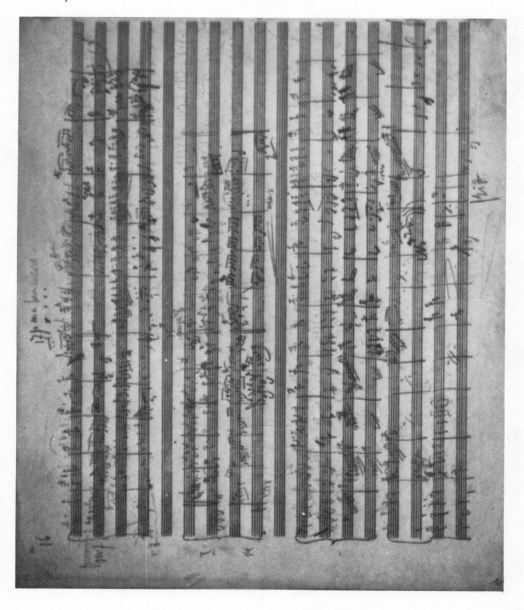

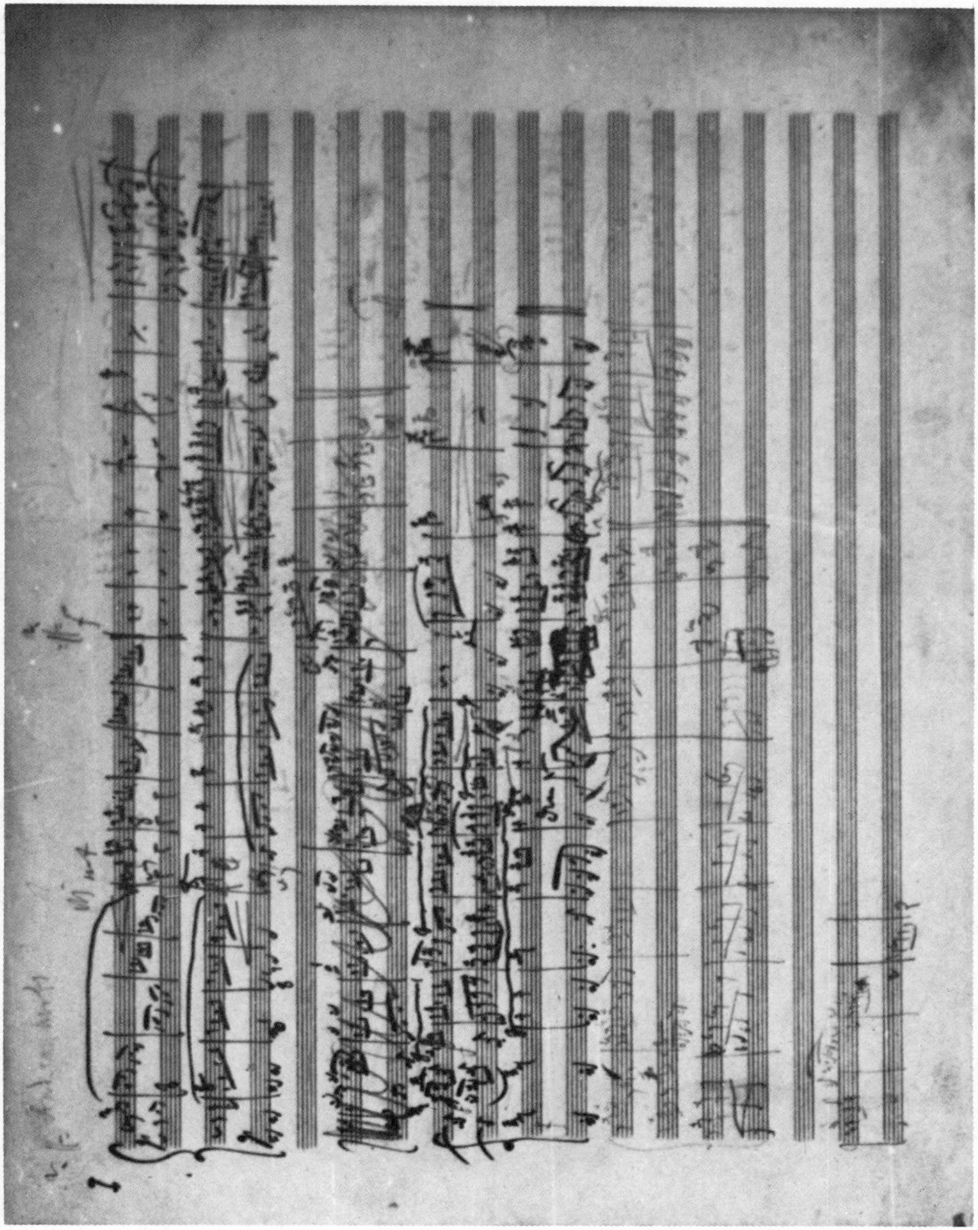

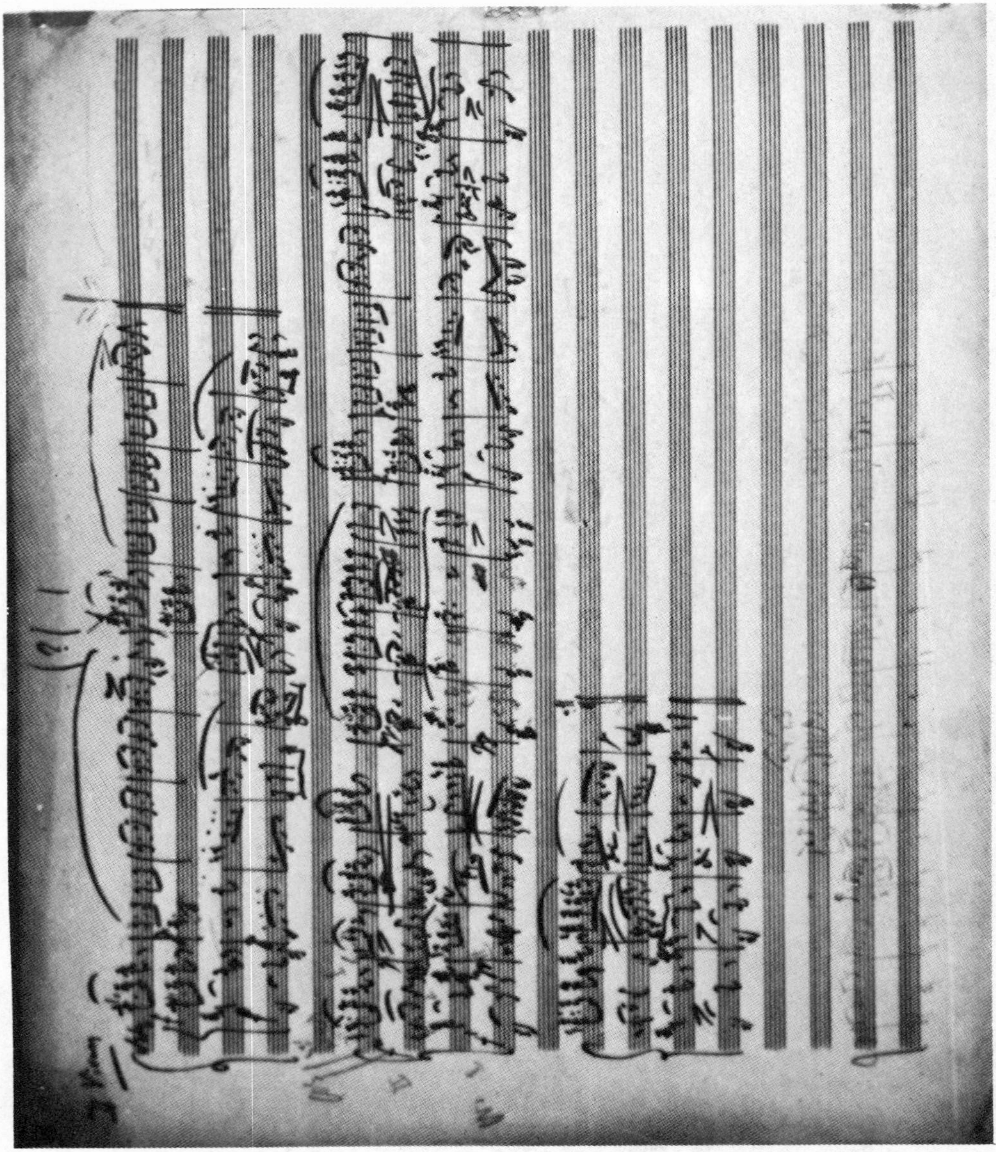

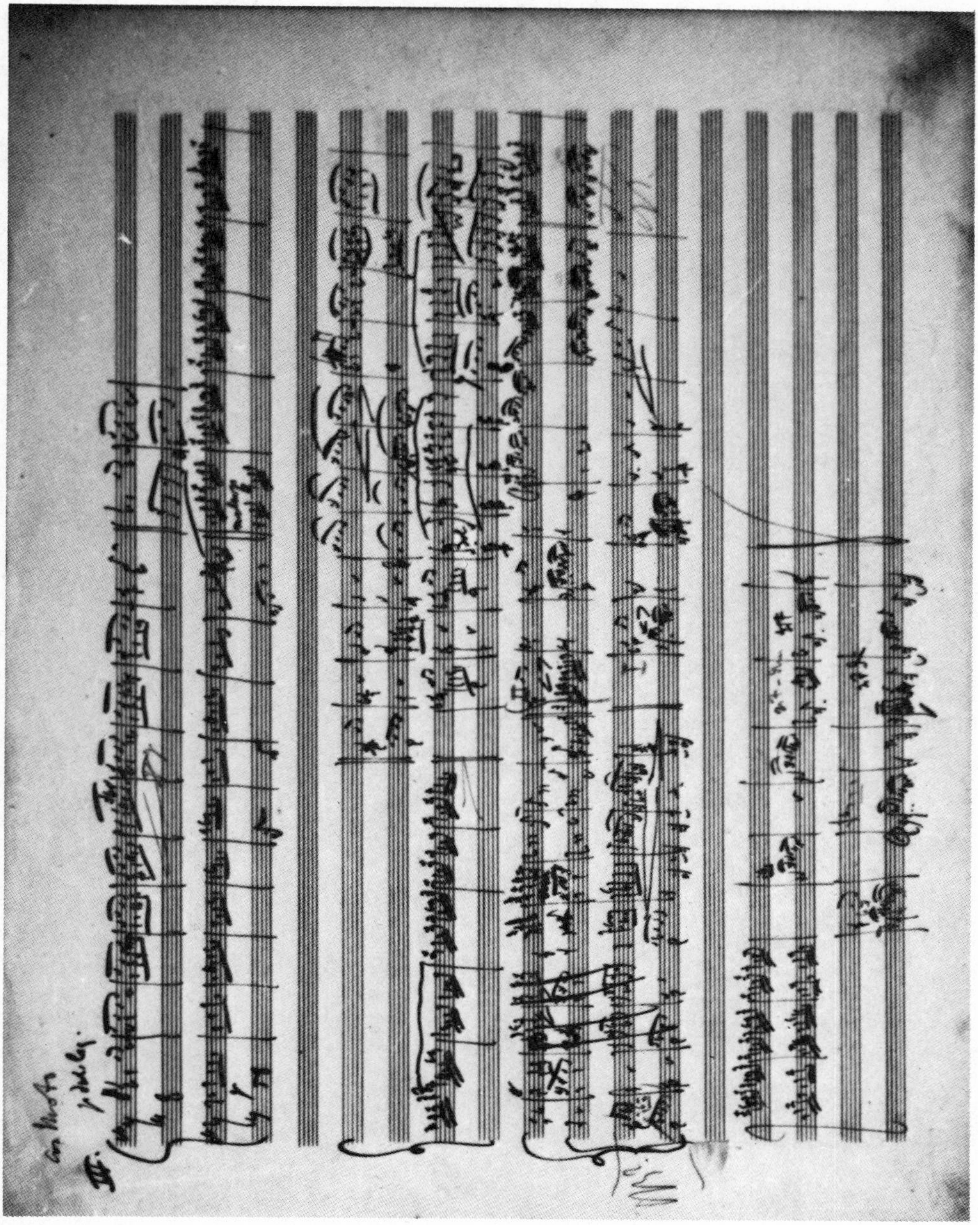

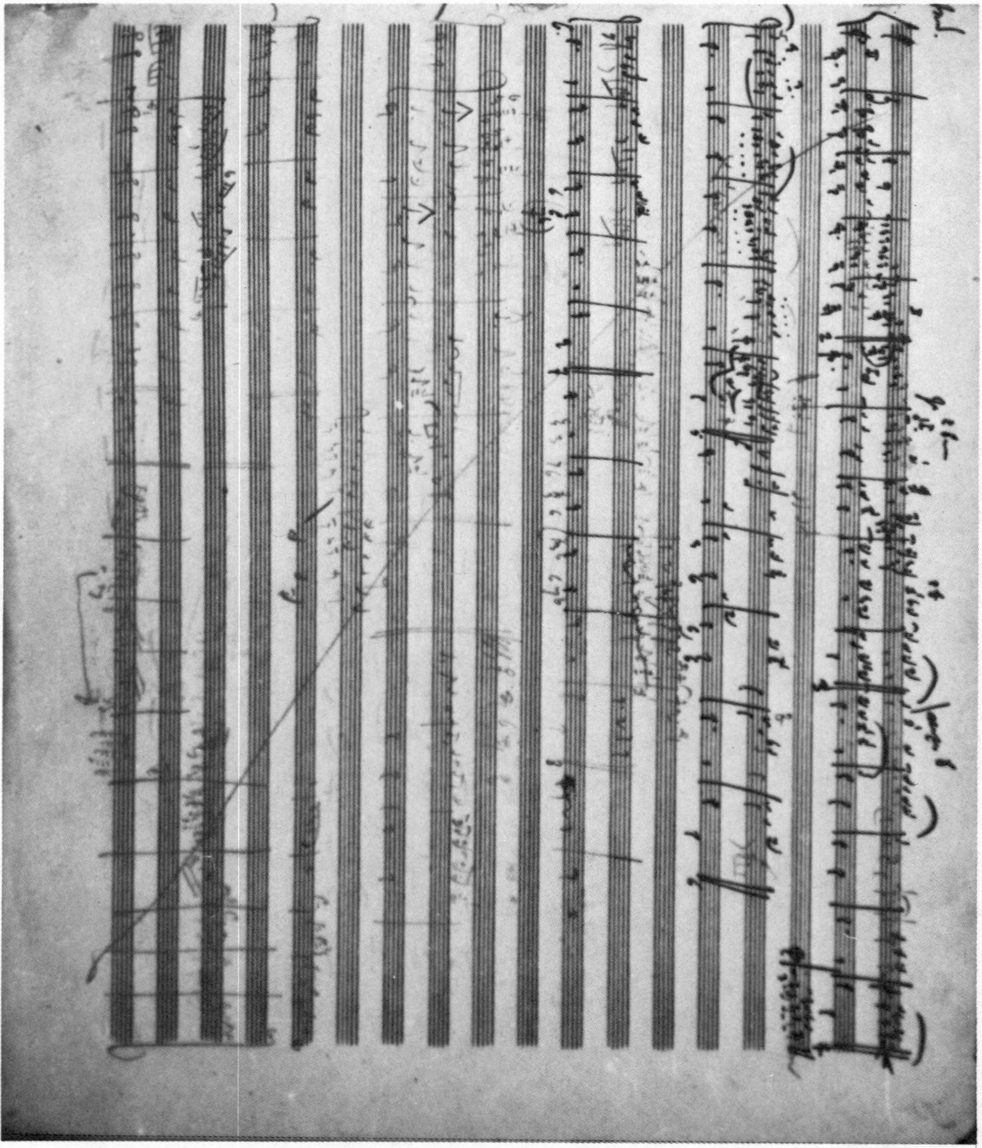

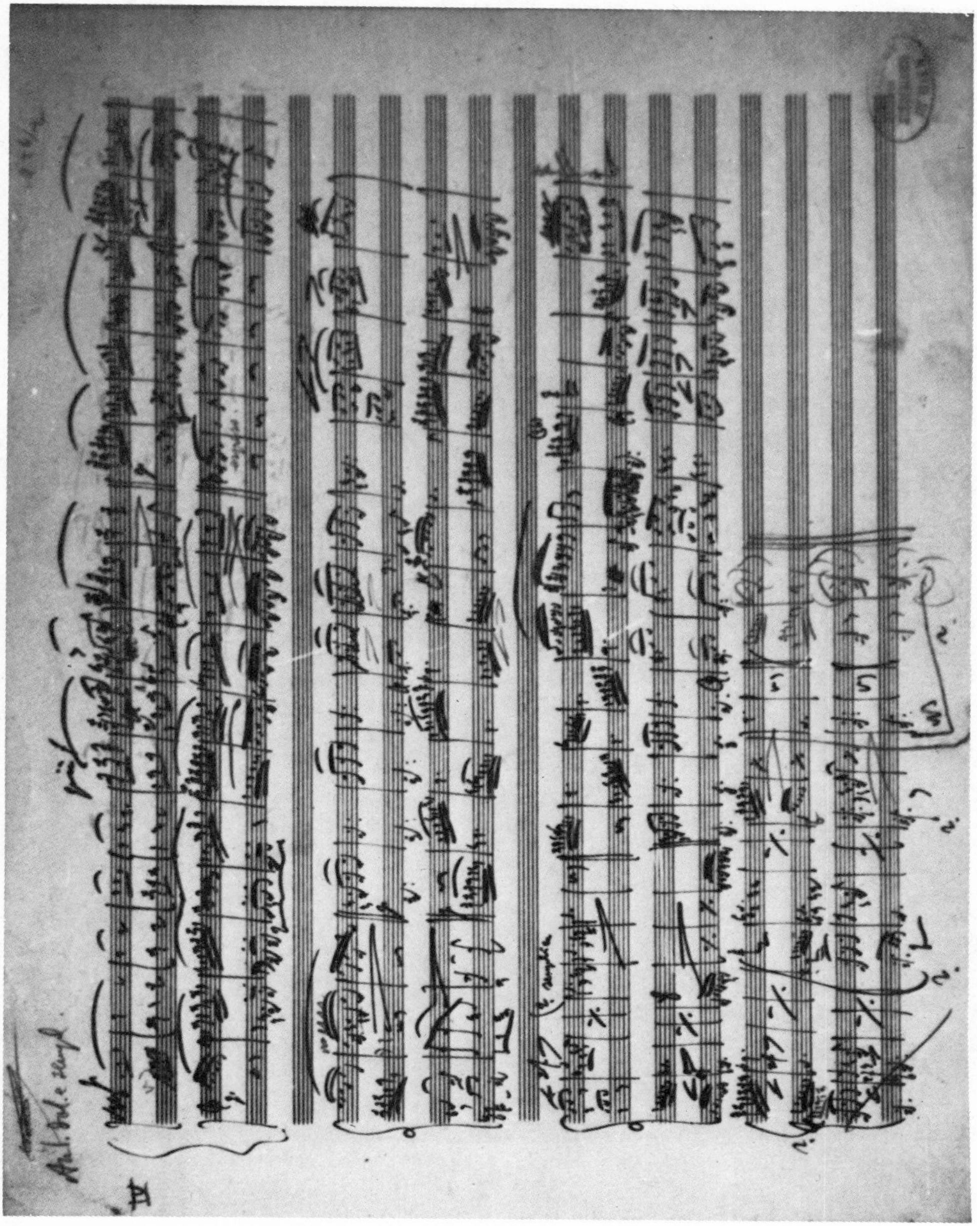

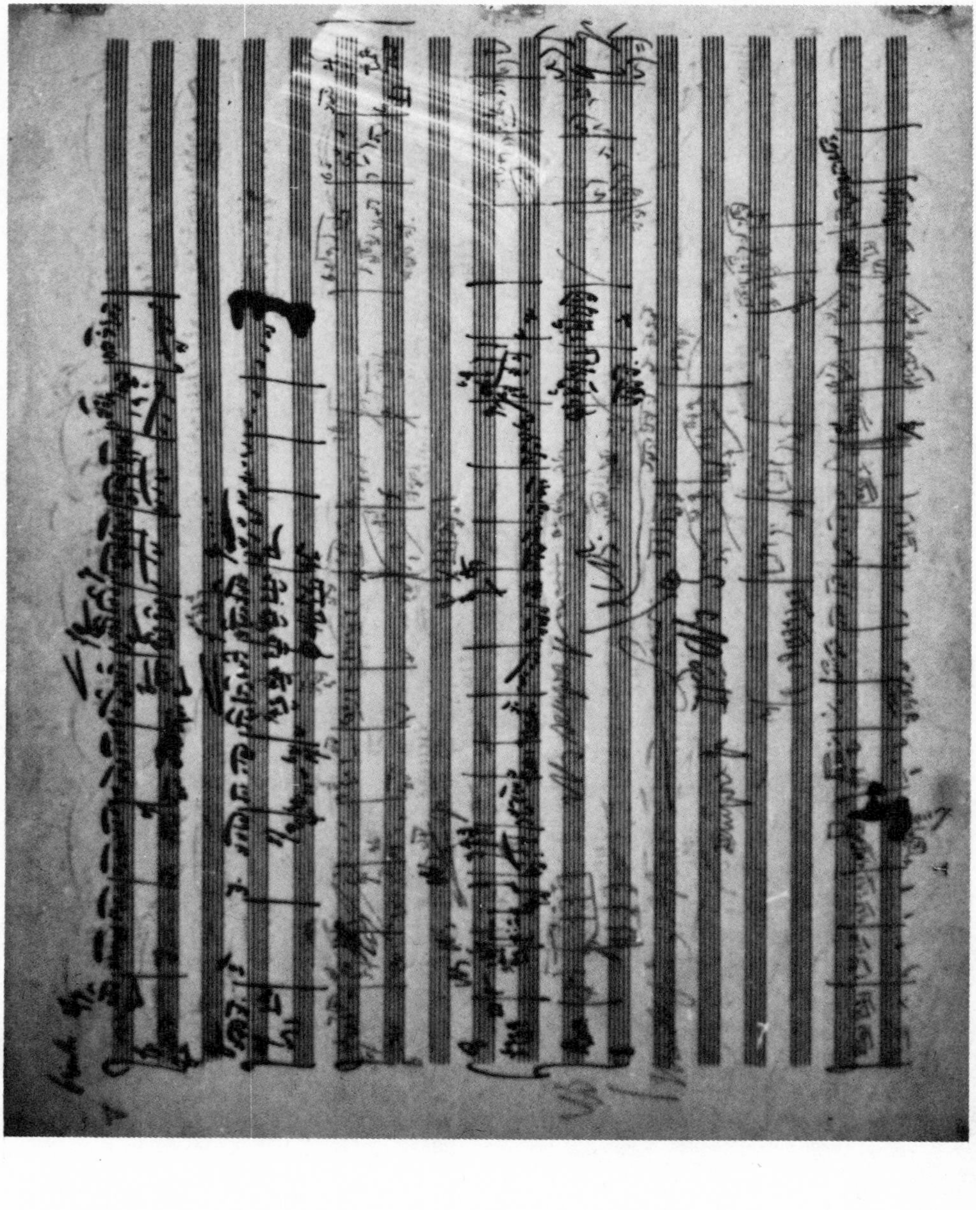

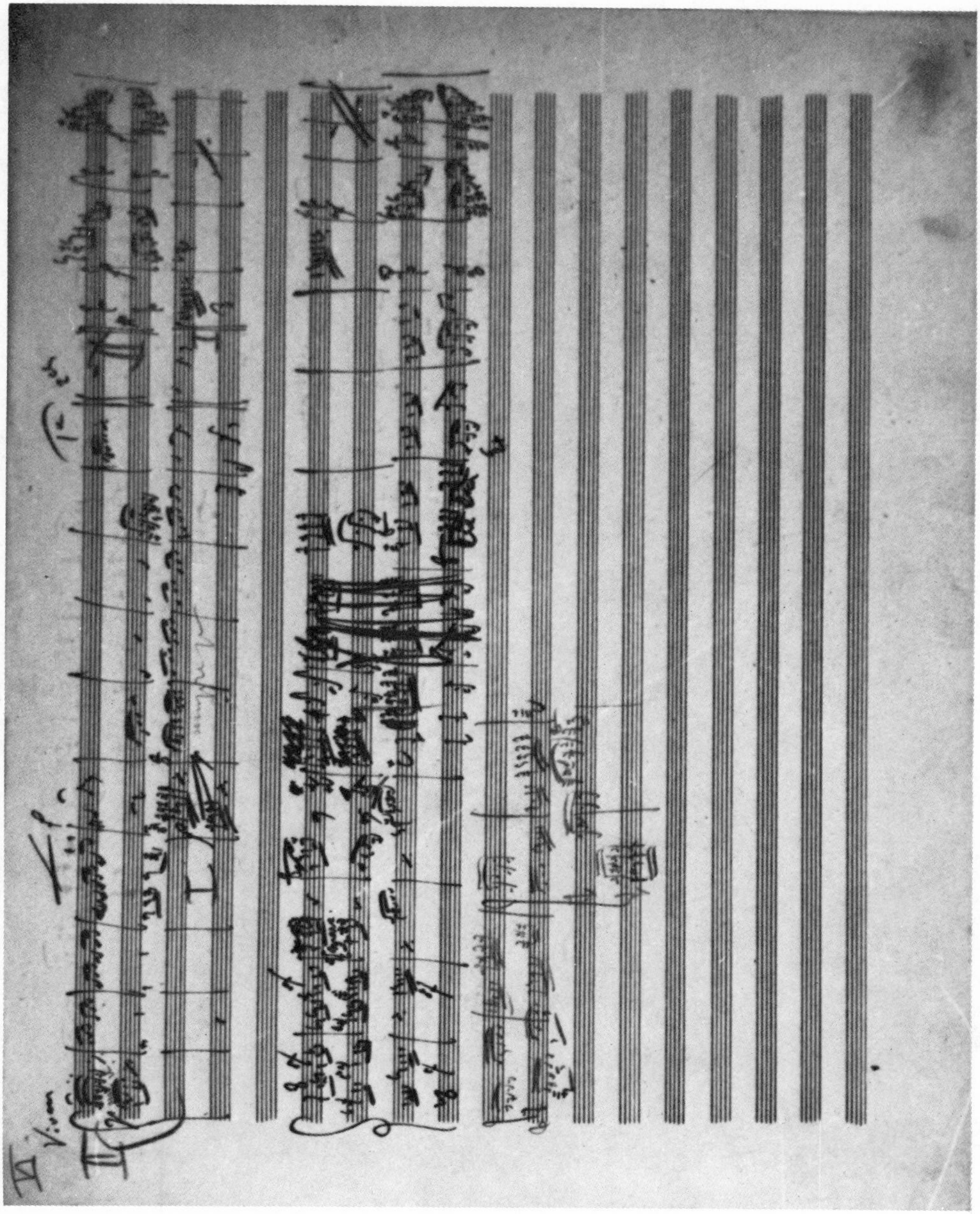

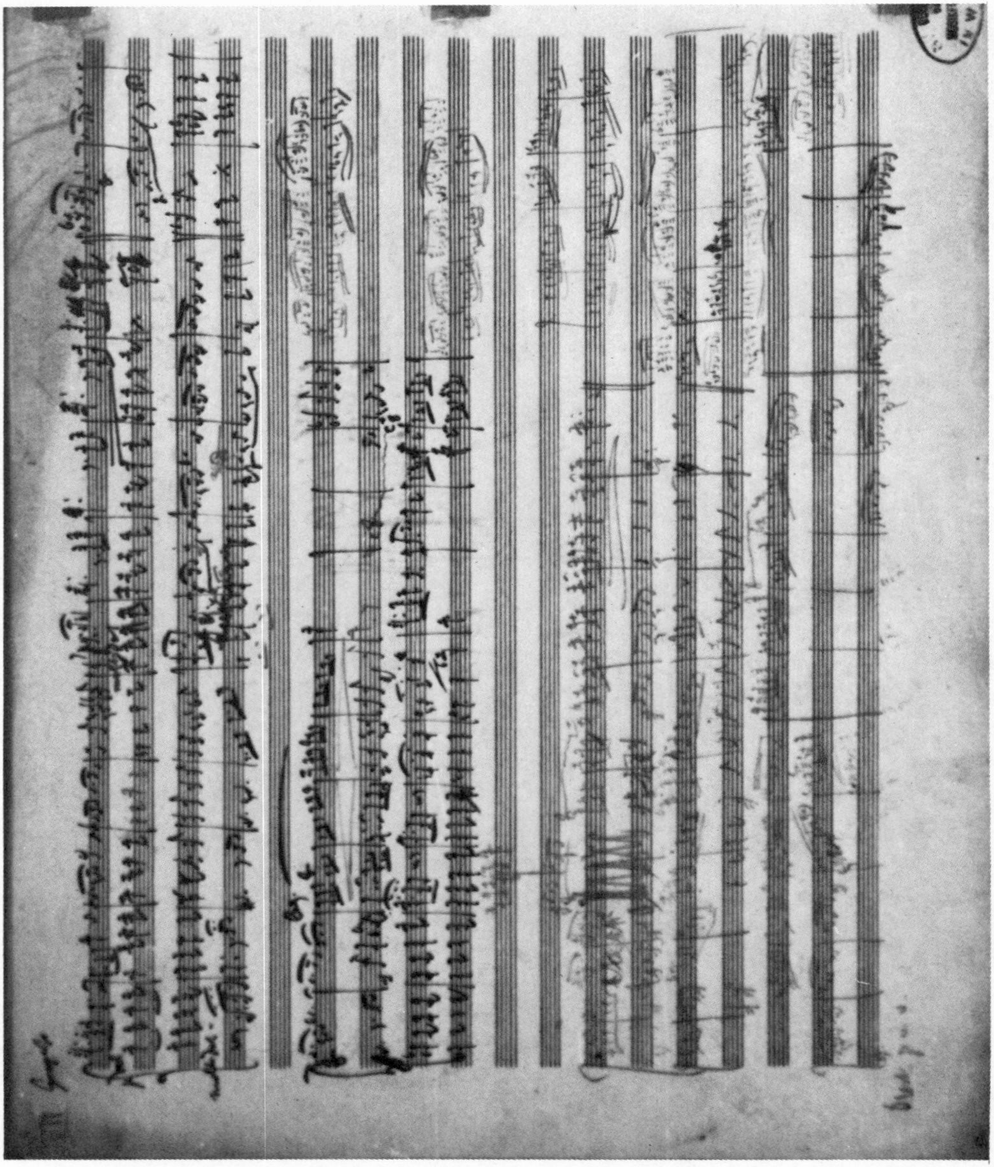

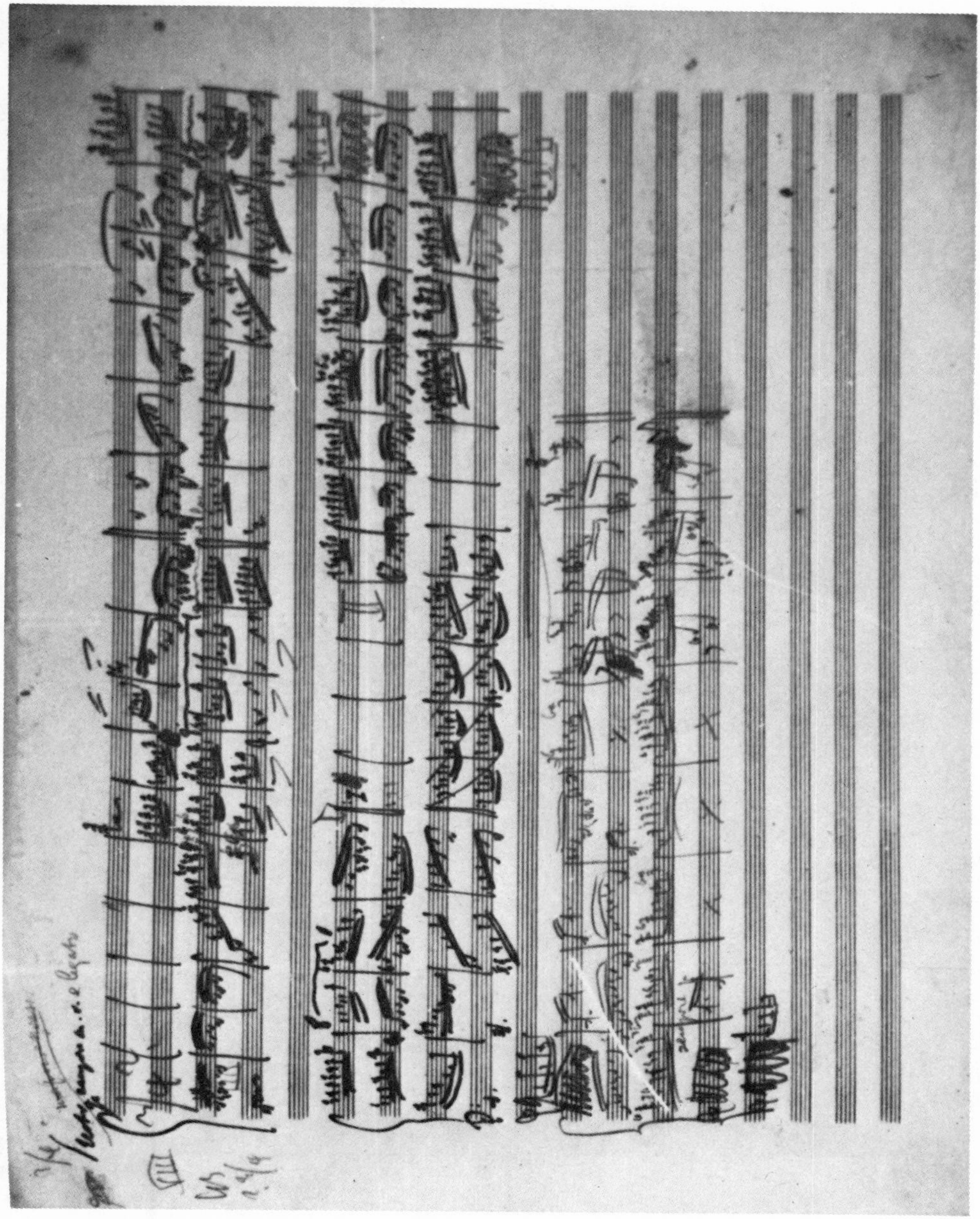

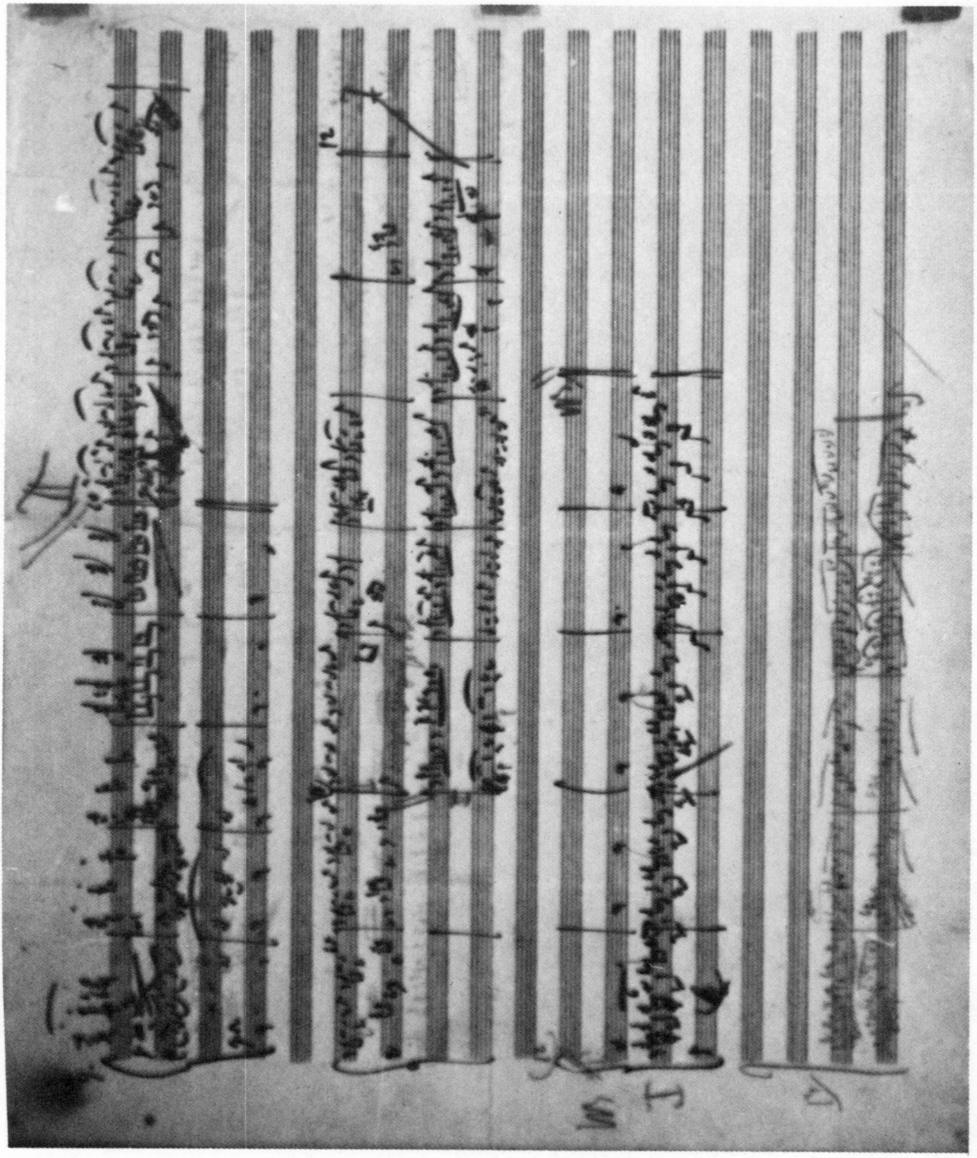

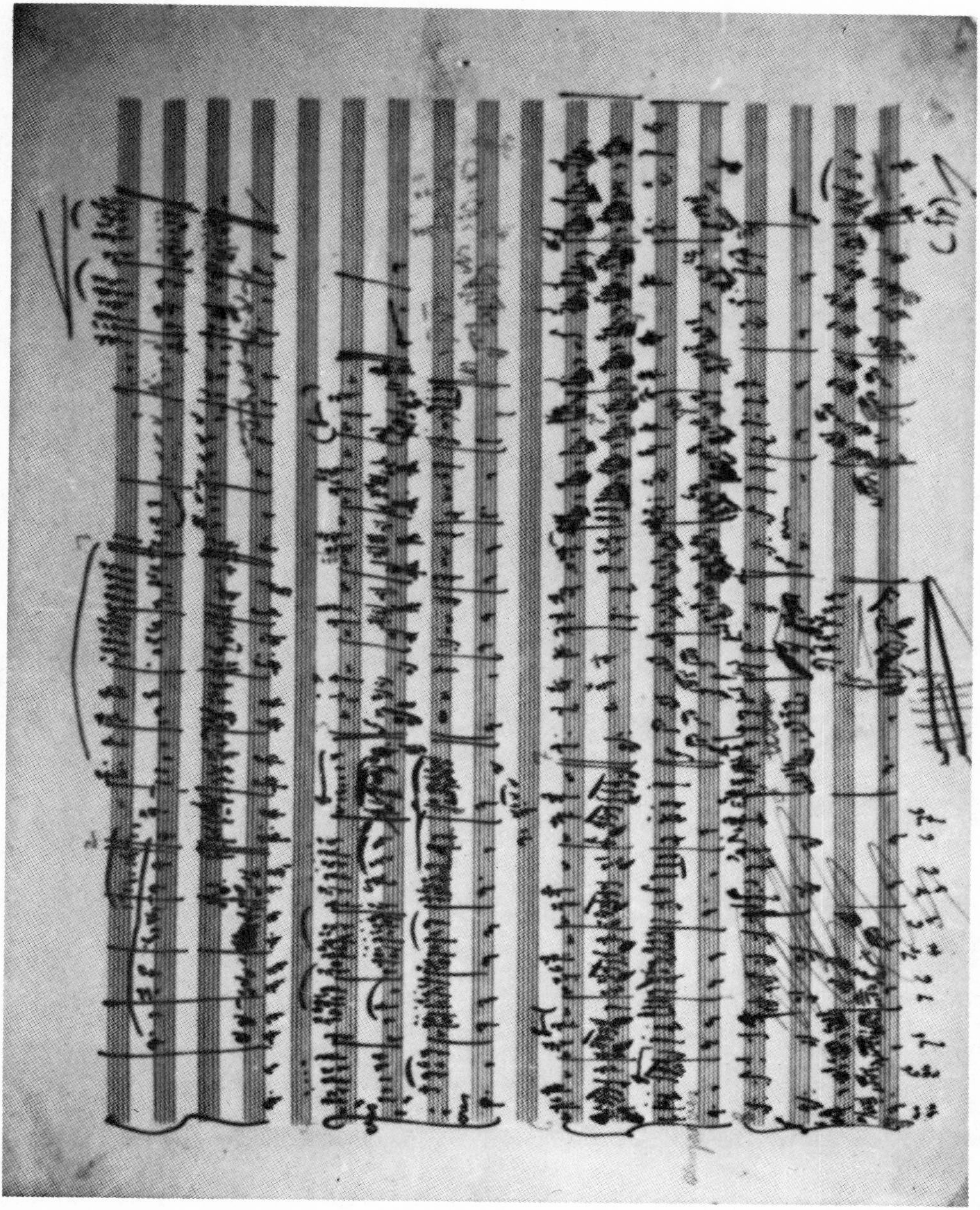

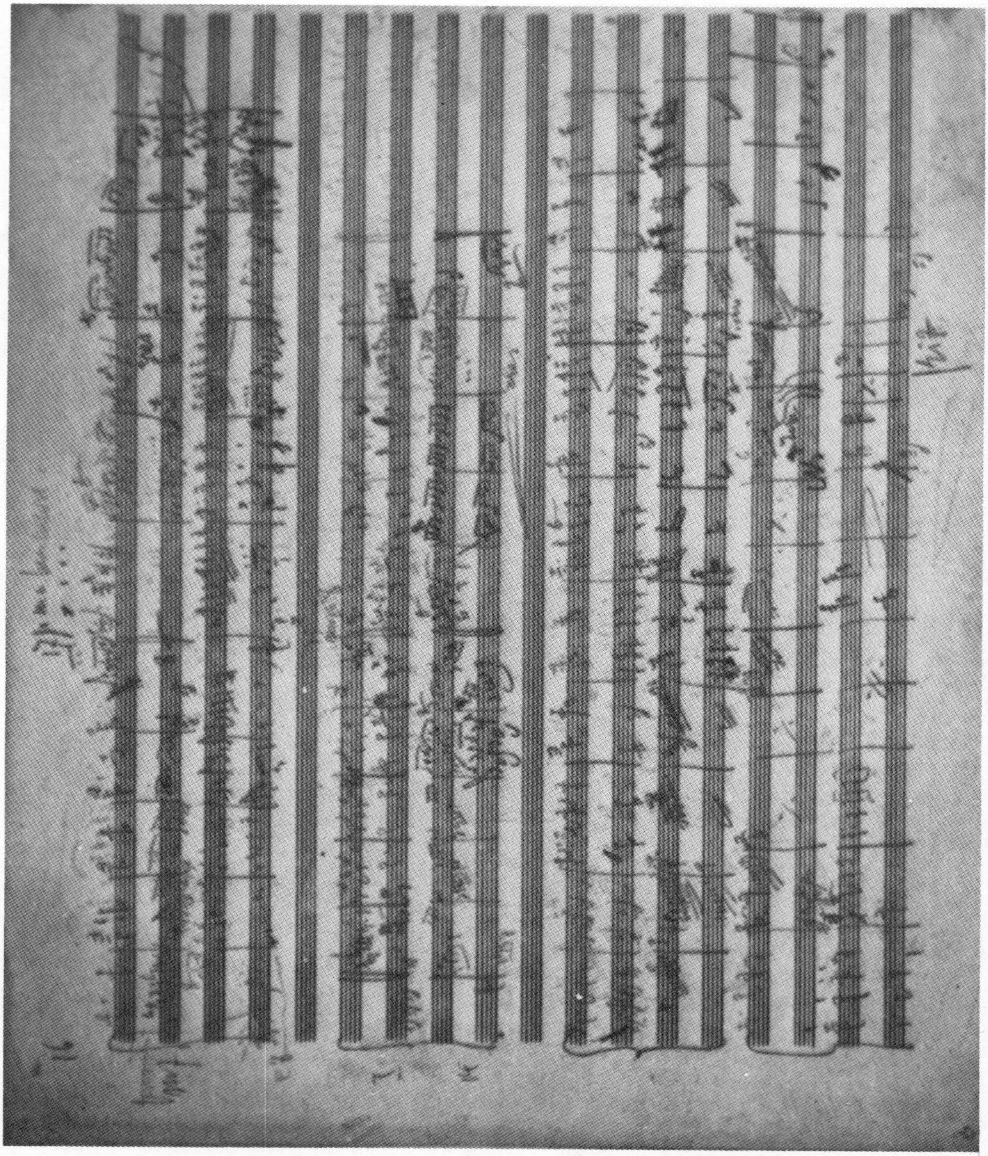

Textual Criticism and Notes

The present scores are based on the texts of the respective editions in the *Johannes Brahms Sämtliche Werke. Ausgabe der Gesellschaft der Musikfreunde in Wien* [Johannes Brahms's Collected Works. Edition of the Society of Friends of Music in Vienna], Vol. 3 (Op. 56a) and Vol. 11 (Op. 56b), Leipzig, Breitkopf & Härtel, 1926–28. The complete *Sämtliche Werke* was reprinted in 1949 by J. W. Edwards (Ann Arbor, Michigan) and reissued in 1964 by Breitkopf & Härtel (Wiesbaden). Separate scores of both versions of the *Haydn Variations* were subsequently issued by both branches of Breitkopf & Härtel (Wiesbaden and Leipzig) in the *Partitur-Bibliothek* series (No. 3203 for Op. 56a) and *Edition Breitkopf* series (No. 6058 for Op. 56b), although it is probable that not all notational details are precisely the same in the apparently identical prints. The identity of the original editors, Eusebius Mandyczewski[1] and Hans Gál,[2] unfortunately was not included in the separate scores; otherwise these issues are virtually the same as the original Collected Works editions, the only other differences being a few minor corrections and some new errors which have inexplicably crept in.

For this Norton Critical Score the present editor has collated each of the editions and issues to confirm the accuracy of the musical texts reprinted here. His subsequent emendations—derived entirely from textual criticism studies of the original sources—are tacitly incorporated in the

1. Eusebius Mandyczewski (1857–1929) was a student of Nottebohm, Hanslick, and the pianist Robert Fuchs. In 1887 he succeeded Pohl as archivist of the Gesellschaft der Musikfreunde, a position which he held for the rest of his career. He was also on the faculty of the Vienna Conservatorium. As a musicologist, he was also an editor of the Collected Editions of the works of Haydn, Bach, and Beethoven, as well as general editor of the original Schubert Edition. He was a close friend of Brahms in the composer's later years.

2. Hans Gál (b. 1890), a composer, was a student of Mandyczewski and Guido Adler at the University of Vienna, then lectured there (1919–29). He was director of the Musikhochschule in Mainz for four years, after which he was back in Vienna as a university lecturer and conductor of several ensembles until the *Anschluss,* when he moved to Edinburgh, where he joined the University faculty in 1945. The first edition of his book on Brahms appeared in Germany in 1961.

scores and detailed in the Critical Reports section below. In editing the present scores he has chosen to revise the Mandyczewski and Gál editions, rather than prepare new editions, because the musical texts established by the original editors have been considered the most authoritative available (though the editorial matter is incomplete by modern scholarly standards) and are essential sources for the study and performance of Brahms's music. The objectives are threefold: (1) to establish by textual criticism the authenticity of the two editions; (2) to complement the work of Mandyczewski and Gál by supplementing it with the editorial data modern scholars and performers have come to expect to facilitate a critical study; and (3) to revise the scores as necessary by restoring and correcting textual details which are lacking or erroneous in the collected works editions. All together, the goal has been to give this Norton Critical Score the most complete and reliable texts of the *Haydn Variations* published.

The Collected Works editions, in general, are reliable texts for what Brahms might have wished to represent the definitive standard versions of his works. But because of the editorial philosophy which generally prevailed in the 1920s, we are unable to know the exact editorial procedures followed by the original editors without making our own comparisons of their editions with the textual sources they used. For in the Mandyczewski and Gál editions we are confronted with (1) scores in which all editorial emendations have been tacitly supplied—i.e., without critical devices such as brackets or parentheses, etc.—which makes it impossible to see what revisions have been incorporated; and (2) Editorial Reports which are uneven at best, and in general cannot be considered bibliographically precise with respect to the identification and description of textual sources, or adequate as reports of editorial revisions. Thus we are not told what and where original details have been omitted or supplied in the editorial synthesis of the several sources for each work. The *Haydn Variations* in the Collected Works editions are rather typically illustrative of the problem.[3]

THE COLLECTED EDITION SOURCES

The sources used by Gál (Op. 56a) and Mandyczewski (Op. 56b) for their editions are described in the Editorial Reports (*Revisionsberichte*) as follows, in partial translation:

For Op. 56a:

1. The Simrock score (title: *Variationen über ein Thema von Jos. Haydn für Orchester von Johannes Brahms.* Op. 56a.) Publisher's No. 7395.
2. Brahms's personal copy [*Handexemplar*] of the score, in the possession of the Gesellschaft der Musikfreunde in Vienna.
3. The autograph [*Original-Handschrift*] of the score, in the possession of the publisher N. Simrock in Berlin.

3. See McCorkle, "Five Fundamental Obstacles in Brahms Source Research," *Acta musicologica,* XLVIII/2 (1976), for an analysis of the quality of the *Johannes Brahms Sämtliche Werke.*

For Op. 56b:

1. Brahms's autograph [*Original-Handschrift*], in the possession of the Stadtbibliothek, Vienna. Ten leaves, 18-staff music paper in oblong format. On the first page the title, *Variationen über ein Thema von Jos. Haydn. Joh^s Brahms.* At the end, "Tutzing, Juli 1874."[4] On the wrapper that covers the autograph in [Philipp] Spitta's hand: "Variationen über ein Thema von J. Haydn für zwei Pianoforte von Johannes Brahms (Autograph)." Beneath that, "(Geschenk des Komponisten [Gift of the composer] Dec. 1873) Philipp Spitta."

2. The composer's personal copy [*Handexemplar*] of the first edition in the possession of the Gesellschaft der Musikfreunde in Vienna. This edition appeared under the title *Variationen über ein Thema von Joseph Haydn für zwei Pianoforte von Johannes Brahms. Op. 56^b. Preis 4½ Mark. Verlag und Eigenthum von N. Simrock in Berlin 1873.*

In their Editorial Reports the original editors presented only the briefest of notes on their work. Inexplicably, Gál remarked that the Simrock edition "is flawless, apart from nonessential carelessnesses," and identified merely one missing dynamic mark and one misprint in the entire score. Mandyczewski, astonishingly, remarked that "the autograph, which did not serve as the engraver's layout for the first edition, deviates nonessentially in several places from the latter. For us, the first edition was authoritative, and [also] the corrections which Brahms subsequently recorded in his personal copy." Two minor corrections were identified.

It becomes clear when one makes a painstaking textual comparison of their sources that the actual musical notes are the same in each, with a few exceptions; but dynamics, articulation, and phrasing are often inconsistent, erroneously placed, or lacking in one source or another. It becomes clear also that the editors overstated the completeness and reliability of their sources, did not explain their procedures in treating the sources, and wholly minimized the great amount of editorial selectivity and revising they were actually required to do. Consequently, we are left with some important questions about the sources for the Collected Works editions.

A few of these questions should give us concern here. First, Gál did not explain why he consulted *two* copies of the first edition—do they differ beyond Brahms's single correction in his personal copy? Further, how did he view the edition as "flawless, apart from nonessential carelessnesses"—did he mean that there were no errors in the musical notes, but that the carelessnesses were found only in expression details?[5] Nor did he mention to what extent he may have relied upon the autograph—the one and only draft of the score—for his revisions. Second, Mandyczewski's statement that

4. "1874" is surely a misprint, for "1873" is the date that actually appears in the autograph.

5. Recently (1975) Hans Gál expressed to me his conviction that the explicit structural details of a work (tones, rhythm, form, etc.) are the essential elements, and the implicit details of expression amount to nonessentials. (This view is discussed in McCorkle, *ibid.*)

the first edition was authoritative for his work would appear to contradict his citation of the autograph as his principal source. Actually, the first autograph *does* deviate from the edition significantly (if not "essentially"), chiefly because the edition in fact is badly flawed by errors and omissions.[6] How then did he use the edition as an "authoritative" text? If he did use it as his basis, his task was more difficult than he admitted, in consideration of the many discrepancies and inconsistencies in the edition. On the other hand, if he used the autograph as a basis, his work was facilitated by a more reliable, though unpolished text which he (better than anyone) should have been readily able to complete, by virtue of his intimate knowledge of Brahms's style and characteristic treatment of expression details. Probably we will never know specifically how the edition was prepared—the Breitkopf & Härtel engraver's copies for the Collected Works are not known to be extant[7]—but it is easy to see that the edition collates best with the much more reliable part-autograph (the manuscript originally used as engraver's layout by N. Simrock), which he did not even include among his sources!

THE COMPLETE SOURCES

Following are the present editor's descriptions of four of the five sources cited by Gál and Mandyczewski, expanded to conform essentially with modern bibliographical practice, together with a description of the additional source (part-autograph) not included among their sources. These will appear in the order as cited in the Editorial Reports (see above), beginning with No. 2; No. 1, the extra first edition, being redundant, is omitted here. The acronyms supplied—*SEHE, AMS, PAMS*—will be used to identify the sources that document the revisions of each editor, as detailed in the Critical Reports below. The numeral after each acronym indicates the probable genealogical position of each manuscript and printed

6. The first (score) edition actually replaced the aborted original first edition, which was not distributed widely because Brahms vehemently protested its format as separate parts (*Primo* and *Secondo*), more appropriate for piano duet than for two pianos. (A copy of this very rare withdrawn print is owned by the British Museum, London.) Brahms was very busy at the time, so probably he did not bother to read the rejected parts, which he insisted had to be reengraved in score format (letter, November 10, 1873, in *Johannes Brahms Briefwechsel,* 16 vols. [Berlin, 1908–22; repr. Tutzing, 1974], IX, pp. 155–57). We may surmise from a comparison of the authentic first edition and the part-autograph that he never did correct proofs for the score edition.

In recent years the problem of identifying the authentic first (score) edition has been made more complicated for the nonspecialist by the publication of a reprint from N. Simrock (London-Hamburg). The reprint (Elite Edition, imprint A. L. & Co. Ltd. 3430) purports to be "N. Simrock's Original Edition," and superficially looks to be such, but in fact is not. On the whole, the authentic first edition, even without Brahms's corrections, is far less flawed than this spurious edition.

7. They were probably destroyed with the bulk of the Breitkopf & Härtel archives in the bombardment of December 4, 1943. Hans Gál has informed me that no galley proofs were shown to him and Mandyczewski.

source in the evolutionary stages from two-piano version through orchestral version of the *Haydn Variations.*

For Op. 56a:

SEHE 2 Simrock Edition, *Handexemplar* (Brahms's personal copy). Title page: *Variationen / über ein Thema von Jos. Haydn / für Orchester / von / Johannes Brahms. / Op.* 56^{a} / [rule] / *Partitur. / Pr. 9 Mark netto. / Ent*^{d} *Stat. Hall. / Verlag und Eigenthum / von / N. Simrock in Berlin.* [Pl. no. 7395. Pub. d. January 1874.] Vienna, Gesellschaft der Musikfreunde (Brahms *Nachlass*). This issue of the first edition is very inaccurate. Brahms noted only one error, but overlooked many other errors and inconsistencies.

AMS 3 Autograph Manuscript. Caption title by Brahms: *Variationen für Orchester. / über ein Thema von* ^{Jos} *Haydn. / Chorale St: Antoni. Johs Brahms.* 46 fols., 27.7 × 34 cm. and 26 × 32.5 cm. (last 11 fols.). Vienna, Österreichische Nationalbibliothek (No. Sm. 4369A); former owner: N. Simrock, Berlin. Used by Simrock as engraver's layout (*Stichvorlage*) for the first edition.

For Op. 56b:

AMS 1 Autograph Manuscript. The wrapper title actually reads: *Variationen über ein Thema von J. Haydn / für zwei Pianoforte / von / Johannes Brahms. Op. 56b. / (Autograph.) / (Geschenk des Componisten. Dec. 1873.)* / [signed] *Philipp Spitta.* Caption title by Brahms: *Variationen über ein Thema von Jos. Haydn. Johs Brahms.* 18 fols., 26.3 × 33.5 cm. Vienna, Stadtbibliothek (No. MH39051); former owner: Philipp Spitta. This manuscript was the first stage prepared after the sketches, and is not as finished as *PAMS 2.*

SEHE 1 Simrock Edition, *Handexemplar* (Brahms's personal copy). Title page: *Variationen / über ein Thema von Joseph Haydn / für zwei Pianoforte / von / Johannes Brahms.* / [rule] / *Op.* 56^{b} *Preis 4½ Mark.* / [florid ornament] / *Ent*^{d} *Stat. Hall / Verlag und Eigenthum / von / N. Simrock in Berlin / 1873.* [Pl. no. 7397. Pub. d. November 1873.] Vienna, Gesellschaft der Musikfreunde (Brahms *Nachlass*). This issue of the first edition is very flawed in comparison with *PAMS 2,* which was the text for the edition. Brahms noted sixteen minor revisions and corrections in his personal copy, but overlooked or ignored many significant discrepancies.

PAMS 2 Part-Autograph Manuscript. Title page by copyist: *Variationen / über ein Thema von Jos. Haydn / für / zwei Pianoforte / von / Joh. Brahms. / Op. 56b.* Title page + 29 fols., 24.7 × 34 cm. Hamburg, Staats- und Universitätsbibliothek; former owner: N. Simrock, Berlin. Brahms's copyist presumably used *AMS 1* as text, and copied only the Pianoforte I part for the theme and variations and both parts for the finale. Brahms then filled in the Pianoforte II part, made some revisions in expression and notation, and added the *ossia* reading in the finale, as well as *in tempo* (replacing *Vivace*) in m. 467. This manuscript is the most correct original source. Used by Simrock as engraver's layout for the first edition and kept by the Simrock family until ca. 1959. Mandyczewski did not include it among his sources, and there is no evidence to suggest that he was able to use it as a basis for his edition (see below).

Finally, it must be concluded from both internal and circumstantial evidence that Mandyczewski and Gál were *not* able to see or use each of the four different original documents which they cited as their sources, but in fact were limited to one autograph and one first edition of the orchestral version, and to one first edition of the two-piano version. The most important documents—as virtually definitive texts of the two versions—were not at the editors' disposal. The probable reason is that these (*PAMS 2* and *AMS 3*) were the property of the N. Simrock firm in Berlin, which at that moment was in heated competition to maintain its Brahms monopoly in the face of the emerging *Sämtliche Werke* of Breitkopf & Härtel. One would suppose that Mandyczewski, as general editor, must have requested permission to see the Simrock manuscripts; however, Dr. Gál has recently confirmed that Simrock did not make available to them any of the original engraver's layouts.[8]

Viewed in this context, the relatively high degree of accuracy of Mandyczewski's and Gál's realizations of near definitive texts on the basis of the several inaccurate sources at hand is most remarkable. Their editorial work was well done, and obviously relied to a great extent on their own musical intuition in lieu of additional sources to support all of their critical decisions in making revisions and restorations in the two texts. As the reader will observe in the following Critical Reports, Gál actually made some forty significant emendations and Mandyczewski made more than thirty—a rather astounding contradiction of their statements in the original Editorial Reports! Had they had the benefit of *AMS 3* and *PAMS 2*, respectively, for the clarifications and more complete details contained therein, the total number of significant revisions (i.e., apart from superfluous accidentals, etc. supplied to facilitate reading) would have reached seventy for Op. 56a and sixty-five for Op. 56b. These additional revisions have now been incorporated by the present editor.

8. Hans Gál, in an interview with the editor, Edinburgh, June 22, 1975. As I have observed elsewhere, during the mid and late 1920s (until the firm was sold in 1929), N. Simrock commissioned other musicians to "revise" some thirty-five compositions by Brahms to compete with Breitkopf & Härtel. "It is apparent . . . that they [Mandyczewski and Gál] did not consult some of the most important autographs, those printer's copies owned by the Simrock firm. (One suspects that, for obvious reasons, the Simrocks withheld these extremely revealing manuscripts.)" (McCorkle, "The Simrock Brahms Verzeichniss," in *The N. Simrock Thematic Catalog of the Works of Johannes Brahms* [New York, 1973], pp. xx–xxiii.)

TEXTUAL NOTES

The itemizations that follow identify and detail the revisions made by Hans Gál (Op. 56a) and Eusebius Mandyczewski (Op. 56b) over the original N. Simrock edition to realize their definitive standard versions for the *Sämtliche Werke,* as well as the further revisions made by the present editor for this Norton Critical Score. The confirming source(s) for each item (except for the items supplied intuitively by the original editors) is enclosed within parentheses. All revisions by the present editor are shown in full-line italics. The latter have been tacitly incorporated in the scores so as not to alter the appearance of the Collected Works format.

Variations for Orchestra, Op. 56a

Theme

14	Ob. II: slur supplied for clarity.
19	Cl.: *f* supplied for clarity.
24	Fl.: *a 2* has been advanced from original position at beginning of m. 27.
27–28	All parts: *smorz.* advanced from position in m. 28 (*AMS 3*).

Variation I

30	Timp.: *p* supplied.
30–32	Hn.: three measures of misprinted part restored from B♭ to E♭ staff by Brahms (*SEHE 2*).
46	Vla.: < shortened by one eighth note to conform with Vln. II (*AMS 3*).
56	Vln. I: > shortened to align with Vla. (begins on second eighth in *AMS 3*).

Variation II

61–63	*Vlc., D.B.: staccato dots restored (AMS 3).*
64	Picc., C.Bn.: portato dots restored (*AMS 3*).
	Timp.: staccato dot restored (*AMS 3*).
64–68	*Vlc., D.B.: staccato dots restored (AMS 3).*
65	Vln. I: staccato dot restored (*AMS 3*).
72	Vla.: ♮ restored to d (*AMS 3*).
75	Cl., Bn.: < lengthened to conform with Picc., Fl. (*AMS 3*).
77–80	*Vlc., D.B.: staccato dots restored (AMS 3).*
81	C.Bn.: *SEHE 2* has staccato dot over eighth note (like Fl., Ob., Cl., Bn.); removed to conform with similar context of Picc. and strings (*AMS 3*).
	Vln. II, Vla.: > supplied.
81–84	C.Bn.: > supplied.
81–85	Picc.: > and *dim.* supplied.
83–84	Cl.: > supplied.
87	Vla.: > shortened to conform with Vlc. and D.B.

Variation III

96–97	Bn.: correction of original misprint, which placed both parts a third lower.
97	Vla.: *p* supplied.
114	Hn. (B♭): < lengthened by one beat to align with other parts (*AMS 3*).
118–19	*Vln. I: > restored (AMS 3).*
123	*Cl.: < lengthened through last note (AMS 3, SEHE 2).*
132	*Ob.: length of < restored (AMS 3). (Originally printed as beginning after 3rd note, revised by Gál to begin on 2nd note.)*
138	Ob. II, Hn. II: slurs restored (*AMS 3*).
143	All parts: general *rit.* replaces original individual indications.

Variation IV

154–55	Ob. II: slur restored (*AMS 3*).
	Bn.: length of > restored (AMS 3). (Originally printed to begin after first note; retained by Gál, except for Bn., where it was shortened to begin on 2nd note.)
196	Vln. I: ♭ added to third note.
197	Bn. II: third note correction of misprint (G♭) in *SEHE 2*.
202–03	Fl.: ♭ removed from first note d″ in both measures.

Variation V

211–12	*Picc.: staccato dots on beats 4 and 1 restored (AMS 3).*
212	Hn.: staccato dots restored (*AMS 3*).
218	Vln. II: ♮ added to c″ for clarity.
219	Vla.: ♮ added to c′ for clarity.
222	Picc., Fl., Cl.: flats and natural signs added to third beat for clarity.
226	Vln. II: *a 2* indication removed.
	Vlc., D.B.: arco indications restored, as in m. 245 (SEHE 2).
232	*Ob. II, Bn. II: slurs under quarter–eighth figures restored (AMS 3).*
234	*Fl.: slur over first and second notes restored (AMS 3).*
242–44	*Vln. I: staccato dots restored (AMS 3).*
243–44	*D.B.: staccato dots restored (AMS 3).*
248	Vln. II: ♮ added to d″ (fourth beat).
251	*Ob. II, Bn. II: slurs under quarter–eighth figures restored for clarity (SEHE 2).*
253	Picc.: *pp* supplied.
255	Vlc.: ♯ before third note (c′) restored in place of erroneous ♮ (*AMS 3*).
257–58	D.B.: staccato dots supplied.
261	*Hn.: > shortened by one eighth note. Diminuendo begins on second eighth for all winds.*
261–63	*D.B.: staccato dots restored (SEHE 2).*

Variation VI

264–67 *Vlc., D.B.: staccato dots supplied (except last note m. 267).*
265–67 Vla.: staccato dots supplied (except last note m. 267).
267 Hn. (B♭): < restored. *Bn., C.Bn., Hn. (E♭): < restored (AMS 3).*
268–69 D.B.: staccato dots restored (*AMS 3*).
275 *Picc.: staccato dots restored (AMS 3).*
280–81 Cl.: all staccato dots after first two (m. 280) supplied.
282 Ob. I: ♭ added to third note for clarity.
283 *Vla.: > restored (SEHE 2).*
283–84 *Cl.: staccato dots restored on third and fourth sixteenths (AMS 3).*
284 Vla.: > on first note supplied.
285 *Timp.: staccato dots supplied on second and third sixteenths.*

Variation VII

295 Fl.: ♭ added to last note for clarity.
300–01 *Bn.: < > supplied. (The > appears in AMS 3.)*
301–02 Hn.: long > shortened: originally printed on fourth beat; begins on second beat, m. 302, in *AMS 3*.
302 Hn.: ♮ added for clarity.
303 Bn.: portato slurs restored (*AMS 3*).

Variation VIII

328 Vla.: ♭ added for clarity.
342 *Fl., Bn., Hn. (E♭): 1º restored to signal tacit on repeat (AMS 3).*
348 Vla.: ♭ added to second note for clarity.
350 Picc.: ♭ added for clarity.
353 Fl., Ob.: *pp* supplied for clarity.
354 *Timp.: staccato dots supplied.*
358–60 *All parts: > restored to begin in m. 358 as Brahms indicated for Picc., Cl., Bn., Hn., Vln. I, II, Vla. (D.B. originally marked at beginning of m. 358, here shortened for consistency with other parts) [AMS 3]; Timp. supplied. Original edition began the diminuendo of Cl., Bn., Vln. II, Vla., Vlc., D.B. in m. 358, fifth note, and of Picc., Fl., Vln. I in m. 359, first note. Hn. began on the barline. Gál compromised by beginning all winds and Vln. I in m. 359, first note, other strings in m. 358, fifth note.*
360 Cl. II, Bn. II: *pp* supplied for clarity.

Finale

364 Vla.: *div.* substituted for original *a 2*.
372 Vlc., D.B.: *unis* supplied.
373–75 *Fl.: < restored (AMS 3).*
375 Vla.: *div.* substituted for original *a 2*.

377 Ob., Cl.: staccato dots supplied.

380 *Fl., Ob.; Cl., Bn.: triplet indications restored for clarity (AMS 3).*

382 *Timp.: staccato dot supplied; Fl. dot restored (AMS 3).*

397 Vln. II: ♮ added to last note for clarity.

398 *Cl.: < restored (AMS 3).*

401 *Vln. II: > restored (AMS 3).*

404 Vln. II: ♮ added to fifth note for clarity.
Vla.: ♮ added to third note for clarity.

409–10 Vla. II: slurs supplied.

414 Vln. II: ♭ added to second note for clarity.

417 Fl.: ♮ added to sixth note for clarity.

419 Fl.: ♮ added to third note and ♭ to fifth note for clarity.

437 Fl.: second note supplied (*AMS 3*); misprint in Simrock score caused note to be omitted.

441 *Fl.: ♮ restored to second note for clarity (AMS 3).*

452 C.Bn.: ♭ added for clarity.

463 All parts: general *rit.* replaces individual indications in Vln. I, Vla., Vlc.

465 All parts: general *molto rit.* replaces individual indications in Bn., Timp., Vla.

467 All parts: general *in tempo* replaces individual indications in Hn., Vln. I.

Variations for Two Pianos, Op. 56b

Theme

5 *Both parts, r.h.: slurs restored to second voices for clarity (SEHE 1, PAMS 2).*

6–7 Both parts, l.h.: > added in analogy with mm. 19–20 (All sources).

10 *Pf. II, l.h.: slur restored to second voice for clarity (SEHE 1).*

18 *Pf. II, r.h.: slur restored to alto voice (SEHE 1, PAMS 2).*

29 Pf. I, l.h.: note in third voice restored (*AMS 1*), corrected by Brahms in *PAMS 2*.

Variation I

48 *Pf. I: first f restored to original position after, instead of on, first note (AMS 1, PAMS 2).*

50 Pf. II: misprint in *SEHE 1* omitted slur from last note (*AMS 1, PAMS 2*).

54 *Pf. I: dim. moved from second note to align with dim. in Pf. II (SEHE 1, PAMS 2).*

Variation II

70 Pf. I: *p* appears in *SEHE 1, AMS 1*, not in *PAMS 2*. *AMS 1* shows > over l.h.

72 Pf. I, l.h.: slurring restored by removing tie over tenor

notes and replacing slur below bass notes (*PAMS 2*).

81 Pf. I: > corrected to begin on last note (*AMS 1*, *PAMS 2*).

85–86 *Pf. II: > restored (AMS 1, PAMS 2).*

Variation III

99 Pf. II: *e legato* in *SEHE 1*, but not in *AMS 1* or *PAMS 2*.

103 Both parts: < shortened by one eighth-note duration (*AMS 1*).

107 *Pf. I: > removed (all sources). Pf. II: > shortened by three sixteenths (AMS 1, PAMS 2). SEHE 1 and Mandyczewski began on first note.*

108–11 *Pf. I: original phrasing*  *restored (AMS 1, PAMS 2). Mandyczewski supplied as*  *in mm. 108–09, and followed SEHE 1 in mm. 110–11.*

109, 111 *Pf. II: connecting brackets for l.h. removed (all sources).*

112 *Pf. II: dolce restored (AMS 1, PAMS 2).*

113–15 Pf. II: < > *in SEHE 1*, but not in *AMS 1* or *PAMS 2*.

116 Pf. I: *p* supplied in analogy with Pf. II.

118–19 *Pf. II, r.h.: original slur restored to include last note (SEHE 1, PAMS 2).*

124–26 Pf. II: < restored in m. 124, extending to m. 125, first note (*AMS 1*, *PAMS 2*). *> shortened by one eighth duration (all sources).*

125–26 *Pf. I: > restored to begin m. 125, first note, and extending to m. 126, first note (SEHE 1, PAMS 2). Mandyczewski began > m. 125, last note, extending to m. 126, third note (AMS 1).*

129–30 Both parts: < > supplied.

133–34 Pf. II: phrasing slur supplied (*PAMS 2*).

139 Pf. II: < > supplied.

140 Pf. II: *p* supplied for clarity.

142 Pf. II: < > supplied.

142–43 *Pf. II, r.h.: original phrasing restored to extend into m. 143, 1st note (all sources).*

144 *Pf. I: > shortened by two sixteenths (AMS 1, PAMS 2). Mandyczewski began the sign on second sixteenth (SEHE 1).*

144–45 *Pf. II: > restored (AMS 1, PAMS 2).*

Variation IV

161–62 *Pf. II, r.h.: separate phrasing slurs restored for each measure (all sources). Mandyczewski slurred mm. 161–62 together in analogy with l.h.*

164 *Pf. II: > shortened by one eighth duration (all sources).*

171	Pf. II: > lengthened at beginning by two sixteenths (*AMS 1, PAMS 2*).
174	Both parts: *poco f* in *SEHE 1,* not in other sources.
	Pf. I, l.h.: < restored (all sources).
177	Pf. I, r.h.: > supplied to conform with l.h. (*SEHE 1*); no > in either hand in *AMS 1, PAMS 2.*
178, 180	Pf. II: *p* not in *AMS 1, PAMS 2.*
179	*Pf. I: sfz restored in place of sf (SEHE 1). [Brahms actually used sf in each instance in the composition.]*
181	*Pf. II: > restored (AMS 1, PAMS 2).*
193–94	Both parts: *poco f* in *SEHE 1,* not in other sources.
197	*Pf. I, l.h.: slur restored (AMS 1, PAMS 2).*
198	Both parts: *p* in *SEHE 1,* not in other sources.
199	*Both parts: sfz restored in place of sf.*
203	Pf. II, r.h.: e♭′ restored after Brahms's correction (*SEHE 1*).
Variation V	
206	*Poco presto* appears in first edition; *Presto* in *AMS 1* and *PAMS 2.*
214	*Pf. II: > shortened by two eighths (all sources).*
218	Pf. II: *sfz* restored after Brahms's correction (*SEHE 1*).
228–29	Pf. I: Mandyczewski shortened < by four eighths duration and supplied >. No crescendo or diminuendo in *AMS 1. PAMS 2* has < extending to fourth eighth, m. 229; no >.
	Pf. II: > restored to begin on fifth eighth, m. 228 (SEHE 1, PAMS 2).
234–35	Pf. II: *sfz, sfz, p* restored after Brahms's corrections (*SEHE 1*).
247–48	*See mm. 228–29 for problem and resolution.*
Variation VI	
268	Pf. II, r.h.: tie removed from lowest voice and slur and dot restored after Brahms's corrections (*SEHE 1*).
276	Pf. I: *f* supplied.
Variation VII	
314	*Pf. II, r.h.: correction of erroneous* ♫ *on beats 4–5 (all sources).*
316	Pf. I, l.h.: ♮ signs added to f and f′ for clarity.
317, 319	*Pf. I, l.h.: second note, quarter-note duration restored (all sources).*
318	Pf. I, l.h.: ♮ added to grace note for clarity.
Variation VIII	
330	Pf. I, r.h.: original fingerings restored (*PAMS 2*).
	Pf. II, l.h.: slur restored (*AMS 1, PAMS 2*).
331	Pf. I, l.h.: original phrasing slur ending restored (*PAMS 2*), *SEHE 1* extends to m. 332.
332	Pf. II: correction of erroneous beginning of phrasing slur

(*AMS 1, PAMS 2*); quarters detached from eighths in *SEHE 1*.

333 *Pf. I, l.h.: original fingerings restored (AMS 1, PAMS 2).*

335–36 *Pf. II:* < > *restored to original positions (all sources). Mandyczewski altered* < *to extend to third note, m. 336,* > *to begin on third note.*

351–53 Pf. I, l.h.: Brahms's exact phrasing is uncertain here and in Pf. II, r.h., mm. 351–52. All sources include last eighth note under slur, but Mandyczewski separated it in analogy with phrasing in Pf. II, r.h., mm. 329–30.

358 *Both parts:* > *shortened to begin together on fifth eighth (PAMS 2), instead of on third eighth as in Mandyczewski (SEHE 1).*

Finale

377 *Pf. I, l.h.: original phrasing restored by detaching first quarter from slurred group, after Brahms's correction (PAMS 2).*

381–90 The staccato dots and accents are from the first edition, in contrast with *PAMS 2*, which has *tenuto* marks in Pf. I (copyist) and dots in Pf. II (Brahms).

389 *Pf. I, l.h.: misprinted staccato dot over first note removed.*

396 *Pf. II: sfz corrected from sf.*

406–16 Pf. I: eighth rests above staff restored for clarity after Brahms's revisions (*SEHE 1*).

409 Pf. II, r.h.: fourth and eighth notes misprinted, corrected by Brahms (*SEHE 1*).

420 Pf. I, r.h.: ♭ on e′ added by Brahms (*SEHE 1*).

422–23 Pf. II: < > originally positioned over notes 7–8, 9–10 (*SEHE 1, PAMS 2*). Mandyczewski evidently interpreted to read as 7–9 and 10–12, but his engraver produced 7–10 and 11–12 (m. 422) and 7–9, 10–12 (m. 423). *Here revised as 7–9, 10–12, both measures.*

432 Both parts: < lengthened at beginning by 2–3 eighths duration (*SEHE 1, PAMS 2*).

434 *Pf. II, l.h.: staccato dots restored under second group of eighths (PAMS 2).*

440 Pf. II: > restored (*AMS 1*).

Pf. II, l.h.: staccato dot on last note restored (*PAMS 2*).

462 Pf. II: > shortened by three sixteenths duration.

Analytical Essays

Unless specified otherwise, all numbered footnotes in the following essays are those of the authors.

HEINRICH SCHENKER

[*Two Analytic Sketches of the* Chorale St. Antoni *Theme*]†

Heinrich Schenker (1867–1935) came upon the Viennese musical scene at a time when traditional concepts and values in the arts and sciences were in the throes of upheaval through the efforts of the young intellectuals of the *fin de siècle,* and diagnostic analysis was everywhere in the air. Although his own musical ambience remained essentially rooted in tonal music, his brilliant analytical insights were perhaps influenced by the current trends toward introspection and psychoanalysis. A student of Bruckner, he was nevertheless very fond of Brahms's music and made some important contributions to our understanding through studies of several works as well as theoretical problems faced by the composer. It is believed that Brahms recommended Schenker's compositions to his own publisher, N. Simrock, and Professor Oswald Jonas has said that Schenker spoke of Brahms as "the last great German composer."

CHORALE ST. ANTONI [MELODIC-HARMONIC ANALYSIS][1]

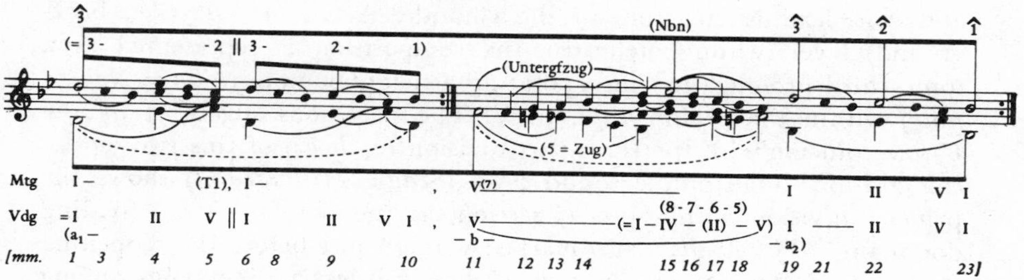

CHORALE ST. ANTONI [RHYTHMIC ANALYSIS]

† From *Der freie Satz* (*Neue Musikalische Theorien und Phantasien,* 3), *Anhang: Figurentafeln* (Vienna, 1935), Fig. 42, 2; Fig. 138, 3. Used by permission of Universal Edition A.G., Wien.

1. For an explanation of the German abbreviations, as well as of the analytic sketches themselves, see the following essay by Murray J. Gould. [*Editor*]

MURRAY J. GOULD

A Commentary on Schenker's Analytic Sketches†

Murray J. Gould (b. 1932) first became interested in Schenkerian theory in the early 1960s. His Ph. D. dissertation, "Species Counterpoint and Tonal Structure" (New York University, 1973), is a study in part of the relationships between Schenker's contrapuntal and tonal theory. A recent paper, "Schenker's Thought in the World of Teacher and Student," appeared in the 1975 issue of *College Music Symposium.* Formerly a professional violinist in New York and assistant professor of music theory at the University of Maryland, College Park, Dr. Gould is an editor of the *Contemporary Music Newsletter.*

The first of Schenker's two sketches, which appears in illustration of his concept of *Untergreifen,* gives a fairly complete picture of the harmonic and voice-leading structure of the Chorale. At the *Ursatz* (i.e., background) level (white noteheads), the composition is represented as a tonic–third prolongation incorporating a neighbor note (*Nbn* = *Nebennote*) within the prolongation of V. The partitions suggested by the *Ursatz* coincide with the three-part division (a_1–b–a_2) of this two-reprise composition. The middleground level (*Mdg* = *Mittelgrund*) shows the primary division within the a_1 section, at the point of the "dividing dominant" (*Tl* = *Teiler,* also marked with ||) just before the reopening at measure 6. The foreground level (*Vdg* = *Vordergrund*) exposes, among other things, several compositional embeddings of the *Ursatz* $\hat{3}\ \hat{2}\ \hat{1}$, and of linear third-spans generally. It is both the multiplicity of these embeddings as well as their registral unity that lend strong confirmation to the inferred *Ursatz;* Schenker's reconstruction is admirably clear and straightforward.

Schenker defines the notion of *Untergreifen* in the following way:

† Written especially for this Norton Critical Score at the suggestion of the editor, who here expresses his appreciation to the author for very kindly offering an elucidation of Schenker's two sketches.

Das Untergreifen besteht im Zurückgreifen auf eine tiefere Lage der Mittelstimme, um von dieser aus die frühere Lage zurückzugewinnen.[1]

Untergreifen consists of reaching back into a lower register of the middle voice, in order to regain the original register from this point.

From this I understand the *Untergreifzug* (*Zug* = span or progression) to be a linear span that conjoins a pitch of an inner-voice region with that of a voice region above it; both pitches so conjoined by this middleground span are, in the present case, components of *Ursatz*-level voices. The *Untergreifzug* in the sketch is the span F–G–A–B♭–C–D immediately after the double bar. The "regained" D (as Schenker would call it) is succeeded by an elaboration of IV (the numerals 8–7–6–5 refer to the upper-voice motion relative to a bass E♭), the totality enclosed within an elaboration of V.

Somewhat more in the foreground of Schenker's sketch, it may be observed that this "new" span F–G–A–B♭–C–D can be heard as an expanded repetition of the V span occurring at the end of measure 5, where a succession of these same pitches is truncated within a two-voice framework:

To carry this idea somewhat further: one can, I believe, hear the entire V span *after* the double bar as an expanded paraphrase of a particular slice of the total succession *before* the double bar—that commencing with the portion of measure 5 quoted above and terminating with the assertion of V in measure 9:

1. *Der freie Satz* (*Neue Musikalische Theorien und Phantasien, 3*) (Vienna, 1954), ed. Oswald Jonas, p. 86.

To so delimit the content of a_1 is simply to expose *one* of the possible contextual references for hearing the events of mm. 11–18, a possibility supported by the highly repetitive character of this composition.

The second of Schenker's two sketches provides temporal correlates for the middleground and foreground constructions of the first sketch. In demonstrating that a basic duple rhythm pervades the Chorale, this sketch encourages a series of auditory comparisons that expose functional analogies which both simplify and enrich audition. Compare, for example, the second half of spans 1 and 3, and of 2 and 4; the second of each of these pairs can be heard as an elaborative and temporal expansion of the first.

As a footnote to Schenker's insights, I offer this observation of what may be regarded as the initial step toward structural expansion in this composition:

Staff 2 interprets m. 1 to within its quarter-note D content; analogously, staff 3 interprets mm. 1–2 to within their half-note D content. Modeled in this way, mm. 1–2 and mm. 1–3 may be heard to echo the structure of m. 1.

LEON STEIN

[*An Analysis of the Orchestral Variations*]†

Leon Stein (b. 1910) has been professor of composition and theory at De Paul University, Chicago, since 1931, and was dean of the School of Music from 1966 to 1976. He is well known as a composer and orchestral

† From *An Analytic Study of Brahms' "Variations on a Theme by Haydn"* (*Op. 56a*) by Leon Stein, De Paul University Press, Chicago, 1944. Reprinted by permission. Slightly abridged and edited with the approval of the author.

conductor in the Midwest. Among his works are two operas, *Three Hassidic Dances* for orchestra, four symphonies, a variety of chamber music compositions including five string quartets, and a book *Structure and Style; The Study and Analysis of Musical Forms* with a companion volume, *Anthology of Musical Forms* (1962).

Dr. Stein's point of view is that of a traditionalist composer and theorist who sees the Brahms *Haydn Variations* as a rare balance of craftsmanship, ingenuity, inspiration, and basic simplicity, in which rational logic is thoroughly combined with emotional expression. His essay is an exemplary structural analysis of the components and principal events in the musical fabric as they evolve from and relate to the theme and to each other.

The Brahms *Variations on a Theme of Haydn* is a work in which the most expert craftsmanship and ingenuity are matched by a beauty and an imaginative treatment not often associated with the variation form. It would be wrong to assume, or assert, that every important or beautiful work must exhibit the intricate workmanship to be found here. On the contrary, it is true that the externals of technical manipulation are often substituted for spontaneity and imagination by the merely learned, the pedantic composer. It may even be pointed out that many pedantic works exhibit a kind of close workmanship, and, too often, that is all. However, attention to detail is what ultimately distinguishes the master from the dilettante or from the merely talented. What is frequently overlooked is that preoccupation with detail results from a kind of inner compulsion which the uninspired has rarely sensed, and which the master cannot deny. For, in what we recognize as an inspired work, preoccupation with detail is the result of a compulsion which stems from imagination and feeling, from the necessity for having a passage conform to a pattern, a design, or an inflection which is felt rather than thought out. In a pedantic work, on the other hand, detail is often derived from a purely reasoning process, which may be external to the work itself; this process is *applied to* a work or a passage rather than *demanded by* it.

Although the working out of these variations may seem, on analysis, to be utterly rationalized and deliberate, one soon realizes that the technique is but the medium for the emotion, that this composition has that incandescence which characterizes and distinguishes all truly felt works.

In these variations, the composer has set for himself certain limitations which, at first glance, might seem restrictive. But these apparent limitations ultimately turn out to be not hindrances, but rather means to an end: a broad consistency of mood, even within wide ranges of expression, a consistency that makes each variation an integral and integrated unit fitting into an overall dynamic plan. The limitations are these: each variation is melodically, harmonically, and structurally associated, measure for measure, with corresponding parts of the theme. Many compositions in variation form are much more general and vague in the relation of variations to the theme, particularly as concerns the structure. But here the form of each variation is precisely that of the theme. Despite this, as we shall note, the variations are markedly diversified.

It may seem that the variation form is one which, imposing mechanical restrictions, does not permit sufficient freedom of imagination. But it has always appealed to composers who were not too dependent on extra-musical stimuli, who could find suggestion and potentiality in a musical idea of itself. This does not, of course, exclude the romanticists; though some, like Schubert or Schumann, might seem to have depended on "programs," they never lost the kind of "pure" musical instinct which finds in a musical idea the possibilities for its own development.

Furthermore, the kind of composer who senses profound emotion and has the ability to project it usually has a mentality that employs what often seems an intricate kind of expression, and a kind of technique often found in variation forms. This is not done for the sake of seeming "difficult," and hence profound, but because the emotion demands such a mode of expression. However, the complexities are most often but superficial, covering, but not obscuring, a basic simplicity. Where this is not true, an "involved" composition exhibits that kind of technical fussiness found, for example, in much of Reger's music.

It is precisely in the combination of ingenuity and basic simplicity that these variations are exemplary and significant. They will repay close study by the student; for the general musician, analysis may lead to that understanding which adds appreciation to enjoyment, and insight to pleasure.

THE THEME

* * *

The theme, illustrated below, is a three-part song form. Part I (mm. 1–10) is a parallel period of ten measures; it consists of two phrases, each of which is five measures in length. Part II (mm. 11–18) is a contrasting period of two four-measure phrases. Part III (mm. 19–23) is an abbreviated return of Part I; it is a five-measure phrase, more closely related to the second phrase of Part I than to the first. At m. 23 there is an overlapping, that measure being the cadence of Part III, and also the first of a seven-measure codetta. This codetta consists of a two-measure unit, repeated, followed by an extended cadence of three measures. This codetta of seven measures (2 + 2 + 3) is also characterized by a tonic pedal in both outside parts.

The analysis which follows is that of the orchestral version, Op. 56a.

EXAMPLE 1: THEME

The plan of the theme may be indicated as follows:

||: I :||: II III Codetta :||
(10 measures) (8 measures) (5 measures) (7 measures)

This pattern, with the corresponding number of measures, is followed exactly in each variation, with the slight exception in Variation IV, where one measure is added to the Codetta. In Variations III, IV, V, and VIII the repeats are written out with a change in instrumentation; the melodic and harmonic material, however, remain the same. In such cases, the pattern assumes this guise:

I I ⋮ II III Codetta II III Codetta ⋮

The melodic and rhythmic aspects of the theme which form the basis for much of the subsequent mutations are indicated by the letters in Ex. 1; "A" is the melodic and rhythmic figure of the first measure; "B" is the descending melodic line; "C" is an ascending line using the "A" rhythm; "D" is a descending line using the "A" rhythm, and melodically a kind of augmentation of the melody in mm. 2–3; "E" is the two measure unit of the Codetta, with the a♭ giving a subdominant inflection; "F" is the extended cadence characterized by a quarter-note rhythm; "G" is the bass melody of phrase one; "H" is the pedal bass of phrase three; "I" is the bass melody of phrase four; "J" is the bass melody of phrase five; and "K" is the tonic pedal of the Codetta. Hereafter, when any of the above sections are utilized in the variations, either exactly, or in some modified form, reference will be made to the corresponding letters.

Particular attention should be given to the harmonies of mm. 11, 12, 13, and 14. In each of the variations, the harmonies of these measures, rather than the melody, are utilized. The harmonies, used above a dominant pedal, are respectively, F major (V); a diminished seventh on E♮ (IV$^{4\natural}$); V^{7}; I. We will term this harmonic unit "L."

Finally, each of the variations develops in itself one or two characteristic figures, which are derived from and combined with the harmony and melody of the theme.

VARIATION I—POCO PIÙ ANIMATO—$\frac{2}{4}$—B♭ MAJOR

Part I (mm. 30–39). The horns and timpani utilize the quarter-note rhythm of "F." The first violin melody, illustrated below, is a figuration of "B," the circled tones being the thematic notes:

The cello (+ viola) passage (30–34) is a figuration of "G"; "G" is concluded in the bass part of mm. 33–34. Phrase 2 (mm. 36–39) is the inverted counterpoint of phrase 1, the cellos and violins exchanging parts.

Part II (mm. 40–47). The background rhythm of quarter notes continues, as does the two against three rhythm in the strings. In phrase 1 of this part (mm. 40–43), the harmonic unit "L" is used; the third measure of this unit (42) is altered by the addition of the minor ninth, g♭. The bass melody "I" may be found in the first beats of mm. 44–45, first violin, continued in the winds, mm. 46–47. The suggestion of melody "D" may be observed in the first beats of mm. 44–45, in the cellos.

Part III. Mm. 48–52 are similar to 35–39.

Codetta. As in the theme, the tonic pedal is in both outside voices. The triplet figure is treated in close imitation. The 2 + 2 + 3 division, as in the theme, is maintained. The subdominant inflection is present in the strings in mm. 52 and 54. The violin figure of m. 31 recurs in the woodwinds in mm. 53 and 55.

VARIATION II—PIÙ VIVANCE—$\frac{2}{4}$—B♭ MINOR

Part I (mm. 59–68). The octave leap of the bass in m. 1 is recalled by the bass and piccolo of m. 59. Phrase 1 (mm. 59–63) in the clarinets and bassoons is the figuration of "B" using the rhythm of figure "A". The first violin melody in m. 61 and the viola melody in m. 62 are the contrary motion of the first violin figure in m. 31. In mm. 62–63, the triplet figure of m. 31 (viola + cello) is used. The bass pizz. in phrase 1 is a figuration of "G" without the chromatic passing tones. Phrase 2 (mm. 64–68) is parallel to phrase 1.

Part II (mm. 69–76). The octave leap in the outside parts occurs again in m. 69. Between mm. 70–75 the woodwinds utilize the rhythm and melody of figure "A". In mm. 70–73, the descending figure in the strings, derived from m. 61, first violin, is developed through the modified harmonies of unit "L". This descending figure is used as a diminished seventh chord, sequentially treated in the fifth, in violin I, violin II, and cello. In phrase 2 (mm. 73–76) the descending figure "D" is found in the violins, considering the first note in each measure as the thematic tone. In the same way, the bass + cello part of this same phrase give the unit "I". At the same time, the cello part is a contrary motion version of the first violin part.

Part III (mm. 77–81). This part is like the first phrase of Part I of this variation.

Codetta (mm. 81–87). The octave leap in the outside voices is developed. The two measure unit "E", in the woodwinds, is composed of figures "A" and the descending figure of m. 61, used against its contrary motion version in the bassoons. In m. 84, there is an interesting cadential use of the German sixth, the altered IV^6_5, which resolves to the tonic major.

VARIATION III—CON MOTO—$\frac{2}{4}$—B♭ MAJOR

Part I (mm. 88–97). The oboe and bassoon, in octaves, have a figuration of the thematic melody of Part I. In m. 90, the figuration is identical with the violin figure in m. 32. The oboe figure in m. 88, a rhythmic variant of "A", is used throughout this variation. In mm. 90–92, the horn has an augmented version of the melody derived from mm. 5 and 6. In mm. 88–97, the lower strings have an embellishment of the corresponding bass melody of the theme, mm. 1–10. Mm. 98–107 are melodically and harmonically identical with mm. 89–97, with a change in instrumentation. The oboe and bassoon parts of the preceding period are now taken by violins and violas; the flutes and bassoons add a broken-chord embellishment using the harmonies of the theme.

Part II (mm. 108–15). Two figures are treated antiphonally in the first phrase of Part II. The first figure is derived from the melody of m. 88 (which in turn is derived from "A"); the second is a descending pattern of eighth notes. The harmonies of mm. 108–11 are those of unit "L", except that in m. 111 the harmony is $I^{7\flat}$. In phrase 2 (mm. 112–15) the bass part is the contrary motion of "I". Using, in part, the oboe figure of m. 88, the horn in F has an embellishment of the descending unit "I":

Horn in F (sounding notes)

Part III (mm. 116–20) is similar to the first phrase of Part I, with a slight change in instrumentation.

Codetta (mm. 120–26). As in Part II, there is an antiphonal use of the figure derived from "A", and the descending eighth-note figure. In m. 120 the subdominant inflection characteristic of the Codetta is to be noted in the a♭ (horn in F). In mm. 124–25 there is a suggestion of the subdominant minor. Mm. 127–45 are a repetition of Part II, Part III, and Codetta, with a change in instrumentation. The identical melodies and harmonies recur, but in different instruments. A sixteenth-note figuration is added in the strings and woodwinds. The repetition of Part II includes mm. 127–34; of Part III, mm. 135–39; of the Codetta, mm. 139–45.

VARIATION IV—ANDANTE CON MOTO—$\frac{3}{8}$—B♭ MINOR

Part I (mm. 146–55). The principal melody (phrase 1, oboe + horn; phrase 2, woodwinds + horn) is a modification of the thematic melody, mm. 1–10. The violas have a running figure in sixteenths; this rhythm of sixteenths is maintained throughout this variation. The bass part is an embellishment of the original bass line, mm. 1–10. In m. 153, there is an interesting use of the flatted 2nd (c♭) in the melody, giving a momentary Phrygian inflection.

In the written-out repetition of Part I (mm. 156–65) there is the expected change of instrumentation, the principal melody being given to the strings, the running figure to the winds. The melody is set down an octave, but the running figure is transposed up a fifth, and is now above the melody. The result is an instance of double counterpoint in the twelfth. The same occurs when Part II of this variation is repeated.

Part II (mm. 166–73). The first notes in the cello, mm. 166–69, are f, g, a, b♭; this is the melody of unit "C":

Cello

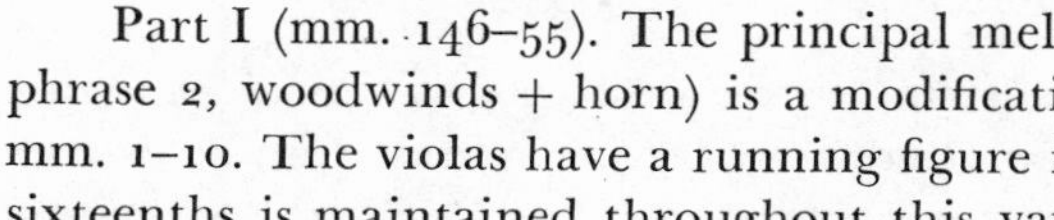

The first notes in the oboe, mm. 166–69, are a, b♭, c, d♭, a third above unit "C":

It is noteworthy that the oboe utilizes the figure from m. 146 (Part I) throughout Part II. The harmonies of mm. 166–70 are those of unit "L".

Part III (mm. 174–78) is like phrase 2 of Part I (mm. 151–55).

Codetta (mm. 178–85). This Codetta is extended one measure at the end. It is the only instance of a difference between the number of measures in the theme and in the respective variations. In mm. 179 and 181, the altered IV$^6_5$, the German sixth, is used.

Part II, Part III, and the Codetta are repeated, respectively, in mm. 186–93, 194–98, and 198–205, with changes in instrumentation. In the repetition of Part II (mm. 186–93) there is a second instance of double counterpoint in the twelfth; the principal melody is in the same register as in mm. 166–73, but the running figure, now above the melody, is transposed a fifth higher.

VARIATION V—VIVACE—$\frac{6}{8}$—B♭ MAJOR

Part I (mm. 206–25). The string figure in m. 206 is the "A" in contrary motion, and rhythmically altered. In the first phrase (mm. 206–10), the oboes (plus flutes and bassoons) play

The arrows indicate the thematic basis. The figure within the brackets is, like the figure in m. 206, a variant of "A". Phrase 2 (mm. 211–15) is parallel to phrase 1. In mm. 212–13 the string rhythm is ♩♪ ♩♪ ♩♪ against the woodwind rhythm of ♩♩♩ ♩♩♩, giving the effect of simultaneous $\frac{2}{4}$ and $\frac{3}{4}$ meters.

Part I is repeated in mm. 216–25 with the strings taking the melodic lead, and the winds playing the reiterated rhythm above the melody. In mm. 220–21, the strings have a canonic imitation of the woodwinds, after an eighth.

Part II (mm. 226–33). In phrase 1 (mm. 226–29) the strings develop the figure used in m. 206. The harmonies of unit "L" are used except in m. 228. Instead of the expected V^7 of B♭ the harmony is E♭–G–B♭–D♭;

this results from the prolongation of the harmony of m. 227 (E–G–B♭–D♭), with the E lowered.

In phrase 2 (mm. 230–33) the figure of m. 206 is imitatively developed in the woodwinds. The flute and clarinet play an embellished tonic pedal, the embellishment being the figure of m. 206. The oboes play the following:

The arrows indicate the melodic basis, derived from "D".

Part III (mm. 234–38) is like phrase 2 of Part I.

Codetta (mm. 238–44). The harmonies, utilizing C♭, A♭, and G♭ give a minor subdominant inflection. In mm. 239–41, the strings divide the six eighths into three groups of  against the two groups of  in the winds.

With changes of instrumentation, Part II is repeated in mm. 245–52; Part III in mm. 253–57, and the Codetta, in 257–63.

VARIATION VI—VIVACE—$\frac{2}{4}$—B♭ MAJOR

This is the most brilliant of the variations.

Part I (mm. 264–73). The horn figure in m. 264 is a variant of the string figure of m. 206. The first violins play a pizz. variant of "B" and "B". The cellos and basses play a slight variant of the original bass.

In phrase 1 (mm. 264–68) the horn in F plays a figuration of the violin melody, using the rhythm . This rhythm, together with the pattern , forms the rhythmic basis of this variation. There is a half-cadence in G at the end of this phrase.

Phrase 2 (mm. 269–73) is parallel to phrase 1, the woodwinds now playing the rhythmic embellishment of the melody. In mm. 270–71, the first violin melody is derived from the oboe variant in mm. 89–90 (of Variation III), which in turn, is derived from the first violin figure in m. 32. Part I comes to a cadence in G major.

Part II (mm. 274–81). In phrase 1 (mm. 274–77) the figures 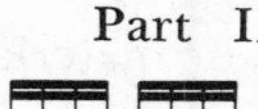 and 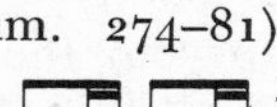 are used antiphonally. The harmonies of unit "L" are somewhat modified. Instead of the expected V on E, the harmony is G♭ major (the lowered sixth of B♭); instead of B♭ major in m. 277, the harmony is B♭ minor.

In phrase 2 (mm. 278–81) the rhythms  and  are combined. The first notes on each beat in the first violins (mm. 278–81) is the contrary motion of the melodic unit "D".

Part III (mm. 282–86) is similar to phrase 2 of Part I. The cadence, however, is in B♭ major.

Codetta (mm. 286–92). In the first four measures, the rhythms  and  are antiphonally used. In m. 287 the Neapolitan 6th harmony is to be noted; in m. 289, the minor subdominant. In mm. 290–91, the melodic idea in the sixteenth-note rhythm is used in an overlapping fashion:

VARIATION VII—GRAZIOSO—$\frac{6}{8}$—B♭ MAJOR

Part I (mm. 293–302). This variation is a tranquil Siciliana. The figure , an adaptation of "A", is used throughout the variation. The notes of the theme may be found in the flute theme (mm. 293–97):

It is a question, however, as to whether the melody was conceived as a figuration of the theme or of the harmony. In phrase 1 (mm. 293–97) the descending scale in the first violins is most certainly a variant of "B". The bass part is an elaboration of the thematic bass "G", in a counter rhythm to the melody.

In phrase 2 (mm. 298–302), the woodwind melody of the preceding phrase is put down an octave into the first violins; at the same time, the counter melody of phrase 1, originally in the basses and cellos, is now given to the woodwinds, above the principal melody in the violins.

Part II (mm. 303–10). In phrase 1 (mm. 303–06), the melodic material of Part I is developed through the harmonies of "L". In phrase 2 (mm. 307–10), the descending idea of "D" is ingeniously figured in the following scale pattern:

The bass part in this same phrase is a variant of "I". In mm. 309–10, the winds divide the six eighths into ♩ ♩ ♩, giving the effect of simultaneous meters of two and three.

Part III (mm. 311–15) is like phrase 1 of Part I.

Codetta (mm. 315–21). This codetta is distinguished by a rhythmic combination of a rare subtlety. The lower instruments keep the basic rhythm ♩ ♪♩ ♪ on a tonic pedal. Above this the violins, and subsequently some winds, divide the $\frac{6}{8}$ meter as follows: ♪♩ ♩ ♪. In the meantime, the winds divide the $\frac{6}{8}$ time as follows:  etc. The melody in this rhythm gives the effect of $\frac{3}{4}$ time, staggered by the barline in the middle of the second beat. The total combination is:

(In most miniature scores, the repeat marks in m. 321 are accidentally omitted.)

VARIATION VIII—PRESTO NON TROPPO—$\frac{3}{4}$—B♭ MINOR

Part I (mm. 322–31). The derivation from the main theme is indicated by the first three measures:

The first three notes are the contrary motion of "A". The arrows indicate the thematic basis of the figuration.

Phrase 1 includes mm. 322–26. For the purposes of the graph below, we will identify this string melody as "X". In phrase 2 (mm. 327–31), the woodwinds have a contrary motion version of the melody of phrase 1.

Part I is repeated (mm. 332–41) with some change in instrumentation and a slight melodic modification in the fourth and fifth measures of each of the two phrases. In mm. 332–34, the canonic treatment between bassoons and violins corroborates the thematic basis of phrase 1:

Part II (mm. 342–49). The dominant pedal, present in Part II of the main theme, appears in the B♭ horns. In phrase 1 (mm. 342–45) the first violin part is a free canonic imitation of the cello part after one beat. The first three cello notes in m. 342 are derived from "A". We will identify the cello melody in this phrase as "Y", and the violin imitation as "Z".

In phrase 2 (mm. 346–49) the woodwinds play a contrary motion version of "Y". The violas play a free canonic imitation of the woodwind melody after one beat; the viola melody is, correspondingly, the contrary motion of "Z". The canonic leader is now above the imitation, whereas, in phrase 1, it was below.

Part III (mm. 350–54). In Part III the two phrases of Part 1 are *simultaneously* employed. The lower strings play the "X" melody, and at the same time, the woodwinds play the same melody in contrary motion.

Codetta (mm. 354–60). There is a tonal pedal in the timpani, piccolo, and horns. The 2 + 2 + 3 division is maintained.

This variation may be outlined as follows:

Part I	"X" — Phrase 1	"X" in contrary motion — Phrase 2
Part II	"Z"—imitation of "Y"	"Y" in contrary motion
	"Y"	"Z" in contrary motion
Part III	"X" in contrary motion	
	"X"	
Codetta	———————	

The dynamic relation of the variations may be observed from the following table:

Variation No.	*Mode*	*Tempo*	*Character*
I	Major	Più Animato	Quiet
II	Minor	Più Vivace	More rhythmic animation
III	Major	Con Moto	"Dolce e legato"—tranquil
IV	Minor	Andante con moto	Quiet, but with a flowing accompaniment figure; nostalgic
V	Major	Vivace	*sf* accents, quick, sharply rhythmic, marked dynamic contrasts
VI	Major	Vivace	Soft in beginning, but soon louder—general character rhythmic, forte Climax of variations before Finale
VII	Major	Grazioso	*p*—dolce, graceful, quiet
VIII	Minor	Presto non troppo	A quiet, subtle, shadowy character; evasive, mercurial, mysterious

We note a regular alternation of major and minor modes made up to Variation VI. The dynamic climax is reached in Variation VI. Variations VII and VIII represent a gradual *dynamic* declension. Technically, the eighth is the most ingenious of the variations before the Finale, and in this sense, it represents a kind of climax, but certainly one which escapes most listeners. It is as though the composer, realizing that the ultimate dynamic climax must come at the very end of the work, and must not be anticipated here, achieved a kind of culmination to satisfy at least himself; that culmination is an intellectual one, one that in no way disturbs the necessary dynamic plan of the whole, and yet brings the series before the Finale to a point of repose and a height of achievement at the same time.

FINALE

The Finale is in itself a set of variations above a basso ostinato, or ground bass, five measures in length. After its first presentation, the ground bass motive recurs sixteen times in succession. In variants 2–13 the theme is in the bass; in variants 13–16 it moves into the upper voices. The bass motive is obviously enough derived from the first phrase of the theme. The motive is set forth in the basses, mm. 361–65, and in m. 362 imitated in the violas.

Variant 1 (mm. 366–70). The first violins enter with a free imitation of the ostinato motive. In m. 367 the flute and oboe enunciate the beginning of the motive.

Variant 2 (mm. 371–75). The strings and winds continue the development of the imitative treatment. In mm. 373–74 the first violins imitate in the octave the descending figure of the motive of mm. 372–73.

Variant 3 (mm. 376–80). There is an antiphony of rhythms ♩♩♩ ♩♩♩ and ♩ ♩ ♩ ♩ between winds and strings.

Variant 4 (mm. 381–85). The antiphonal character of Variant 3 is continued in the alternation of quarter-note chords between winds and strings.

Variant 5 (mm. 386–90). The chordal treatment of the preceding continues. There is a rhythmic intensification in the additional antiphony between the middle winds and middle strings. The figure is a descending eighth-note pattern.

Variant 6 (mm. 391–95). There is a further rhythmic intensification in the inner accompaniment, now moving in sixteenths. The first violins and horns in B♭ have a rhythmic diminution of the bass motive, imitated by the winds in m. 393.

Variant 7 (mm. 396–400). The accompaniment rhythm is now in sextuples, as the *ff* climax in m. 399 is approached. The violins and horn in E♭ develop the rhythmic diminution of the ostinato motive.

Variant 8 (mm. 401–05). The cellos have a pizzicato figuration of the ostinato motive. Variants 8–11, inclusive, are unified by a triplet accompaniment figure in the strings. The first violin melody of this phrase becomes, in itself, a kind of "theme," varied in the four succeeding phrases.

Variant 9 (mm. 406–10). The oboe has a syncopated version of the violin melody of Variant 8.

Variant 10 (mm. 411–15). The ostinato is now in the violas, an octave higher, the cellos having a pizzicato treatment an octave below. The woodwinds have a harmonized version of the violin melody of Variant 8, in quarter-note triplets.

Variant 11 (mm. 416–20). The ostinato is now in a solo horn, with a pizzicato accompaniment in the viola and cello. The flute melody is an embellishment of the triplet theme of the preceding phrase.

Variant 12 (mm. 421–25). There is a pizzicato figuration of the ostinato motive in the violas and cellos, with an antiphonal pizzicato in the first violins. The woodwinds have a harmonized version of the flute melody of the preceding phrase.

Variant 13 (mm. 426–30). The ostinato motive now appears in the oboes, in B♭ minor. Against a scale pattern of antiphonal eighths in the first and second violins, the violas play a counter melody. This counter melody is an embellished imitation, in diminution, of the ostinato motive.

Variant 14 (mm. 431–35). The flutes and horns join the oboe in the ostinato figure, still in B♭ minor. The counter melody of the preceding phrase is developed in the violas. The first and second violins, now in octaves, develop the scalewise progression of eighth notes.

Variant 15 (mm. 436–40). The ostinato figure, still in B♭ minor, is now in the first violins and horns. The violas and second violins develop the scalewise eighths of the preceding variants. Anticipating the return of the Theme (m. 448), the augmented version of figure "A" is treated in the cellos and woodwinds as follows:

Variant 16 (mm. 441–45). The ostinato motive returns to the cellos, doubled in the horns. The woodwinds develop the augmented version of "A". This is the last of the variants of the ostinato motive. What follows may be termed a Coda, wherein a condensed version of the main Theme is brought back; this consists of the first period, and an extended treatment of the original codetta.

In mm. 446–47 the cellos and basses have a rhythmically altered version of the first two measures of the ostinato motive. The alteration in m. 446 recalls figure "A"; the violins and violas have this figure in mm. 446–47.

In mm. 448–57, Part I of the original Theme returns, slightly modified. The modification is in m. 448, in the bass and first violins.

Instead of 

the violins play 

This latter serves as a link between the preceding measure (the ostinato idea), and the return of the Theme.

As in the original, the ten measures of Part I are divided into two five-measure phrases. Mm. 457–71 are an elaborate, extended cadence above a tonic pedal. This section is a reproduction of the original codetta of the Theme (mm. 23–29). The repeated two-measure unit with its subdominant inflection returns, and mm. 461–71 are simply an extension and elaboration of the tonic harmony.

The plan of this Finale is a remarkable example of emotional and dynamic pacing. There is an organic, live quality in the distribution of tension and relaxation. Like any gradual emotional development, it begins with longer swells of rise and fall, which become increasingly shorter, until the final climax is attained. The following illustration of the dynamic plan will make this clear; the numbers refer to the variants in the Finale:

1	2	3	4 5 6	7	8	9	10	11	12	13	14	15	16	Theme	Codetta
p		*cresc.*	*f f più f*	*cresc.*	*ff*	*p*	*più*	*p p*	*cresc.*		*poco cresc.*	*poco più f cresc.*	*p*	*ff*	*dim. ff*

ALLEN FORTE

[*The Structural Origin of Exact Tempi in the* Haydn Variations]†

Allen Forte (b. 1926) is professor of the theory of music at Yale University, where he specializes in music from the eighteenth century to the present, and is distinguished as one of the foremost advocates and interpreters of the analytical theory of Heinrich Schenker. He has also been a member of the faculties of the Mannes College of Music and the Massachusetts Institute of Technology. Among his important publications subsequent to the present study are a paper, "Schenker's Conception of Musical Structure" (1959), and the books *The Compositional Matrix* (1961), *Tonal Harmony in Concept and Practice* (1962), and *The Structure of Atonal Music* (1973). For seven years he edited the Yale *Journal of Music Theory.*

In his modified Schenkerian approach, the author has probed the essence of the composition and isolated some of the most intrinsic characteristics, structural and germinative phenomena which he believes give it its uniqueness and inevitability.

The intent of this article is to demonstrate the interrelatedness of tempo, rhythm, and melody in a single composition, the *Variationen über ein Thema von Joseph Haydn, Opera* 56*a* and 56*b,* by Johannes Brahms. The thesis to be elaborated in particular is that the various tempi are derived from rhythmic configurations which are, in turn, conditioned—if not totally determined—by basic melodic-rhythmic patterns unique to this work.

It would be difficult to find a composition more carefully detailed or more tightly integrated than the *Haydn Variations*. Indeed, Brahms' own feelings about the composition of this music are indicated by the fact that he retained the sketches (twelve pages in all), unusual for him. These sketches, now the property of the Gesellschaft der Musikfreunde in

† Reprinted from "The structural Origin of exact *Tempi* in the Brahms-Haydn Variations," *The Music Review,* XVIII/2 (May 1957), pp. 138–49. By permission of the author and the editor of *The Music Review.*

Vienna, reveal how precisely the composer ordered the work, even to numbering all seventeen repetitions of the five-measure bass pattern in the finale.

Brahms' compositional beginning was itself a complete composition, the so-called *Chorale St. Antoni.* This chorale, in its setting by Haydn as a movement for a divertimento, is ostensibly quite simple, and one might well ask why the complex musical mind of Brahms was attracted to it. What in this music did he perceive that led him to compose the remarkable set of variations so different in style from their model, and yet so obviously derived from it? And more specifically, how are the melodic and rhythmic complexities of the Variations to be explained in relation to the Theme? Even as simple an occurrence as triple meter in the Variations, when there is no triple meter or triple ordering of any kind in the Theme —even this requires explanation in a highly integrated work. We may also ask what organizing forces are unique to this work: why does it have this particular shape and no other?

If these questions are answered, it should be possible to define the role of tempo—the main concern of this study—with some precision; for it is inconceivable that the tempo sequence is a random affair in a composition as highly integrated as this.

In seeking to deal with these and related problems it would seem most reasonable to analyze first the melodic (tonal) and then the rhythmic structure of the Theme's top line, assuming that this line is the single most important element, the element most apt to provide clues to the texture of the Theme as a whole.

BASIC MELODIC STRUCTURE OF THE TOP LINE

By "basic melodic structure" is meant simply the shape of the top line. This is described in terms of simple contiguities, repetitions, etc. No attempt has been made to assess the value of the component tones with reference to the governing tonality. For the sake of economy only the first five-measure phrase will be examined here. This segment, with all rhythmic notation eliminated, is shown in Example 1.

EXAMPLE 1

Example 2 shows how the melody groups itself into a series of three-tone (adjacent-tone) figures, and then into a series of two-tone figures.

Observe that the adjacent-tone groups are enclosures that represent a triple ordering. The triple grouping is thus determined by contiguity and repetition, in contrast to the duple grouping which is determined solely by change of direction.

EXAMPLE 2

RHYTHMIC STRUCTURE OF THE TOP LINE

By substituting the word "rhythm" for the word "grouping" used in the foregoing melodic analysis it becomes apparent that *the inherent or "background"*[1] *pattern in the melody is identical with the inherent rhythmic pattern* (except that the latter excludes pitch). Thus, the rhythmic background can be represented numerically as this series of groups: 3 3 3 2 2 2 2 2. It should be realized that the background rhythmic pattern has nothing to do with accent and duration, just as the background *melodic* pattern has nothing to do with register. These attributes belong to other structural levels.

MIDDLEGROUND

The second level of rhythmic structure, the middleground level, is determined by tonal values (within the traditional tonal system), by duration, and to some extent by accent. Example 3 shows the middleground (indicated by brackets below notes) in relation to the background (brackets above notes). It is evident that the two not only are different, but also that they interact in a specific way: the middleground pattern regroups the background pattern.

1. The term "background" as used here has not the same significance as in Heinrich Schenker's theory (from which it is taken), although it is not opposed to it. Here the term represents a much simpler notion, viz., that any line will group itself according to certain elementary motions. The terms "middleground" and "foreground," also used in this study and also borrowed from Schenker, are closer to his concepts, although readers conversant with Schenker's theories will recognize that a thorough examination of melodic relationships has been by-passed in order that the rhythmic structure may be dealt with more directly in terms of background (inherent grouping), middleground (determined by durational and tonal value) and foreground (regularly recurring accent pattern).

EXAMPLE 3

FOREGROUND

The third level of rhythm, the foreground, is the largest and most stable pattern. Its most prominent aspect is the series of regularly recurring accents indicated by the meter signature. In Example 4 the foreground (indicated by accent marks) is shown in relation to the background and middleground. This pattern interacts with the others in such a way that it is at once independent and interdependent. Observe, for example, that it does not coincide with stresses in the middleground pattern throughout the phrase, although it supports the middleground pattern at the beginning. In fact, the foreground articulates the next to last group of two in the background.

By the coincidental grouping of all three rhythmic levels the phrase is divided into two measures plus three measures. This measure grouping, which is another aspect of the foreground, therefore reflects in a larger span the duple-triple ordering that governs all levels of the rhythmic structure.

EXAMPLE 4

RHYTHMIC TECHNIQUES

The interaction between the three rhythmic levels of the Theme's top line has been described as regrouping. This regrouping, in turn, has two aspects: subdivision and shifting. And although these two aspects are interrelated, they do occur separately during the course of the work. In fact, they occur so often, both together and separately, that they appear to be fundamental types of events, or what will now be called *rhythmic techniques.*

Subdivision and shifting are to be distinguished in this way: if, in hearing two different lines, the metrical (foreground) accents coincide and if the subdividing pattern (provided there is one) consists of smaller values than the other pattern involved, then we get the effect of subdivision. If there is no coincidence of metrical accent and if the subdividing patterns consist of smaller *or equivalent* values (this is admittedly stretching the dictionary definition of subdividing), then we get the effect of shifting.

Perhaps the operation of the two techniques will be clearer if we return for a moment to the top line of the Theme as shown in Example 4. (In examining the interaction of levels in the same line it is assumed that each grouping, regardless of level, begins with an accent.) The foreground here is the most stable pattern, so let us see which techniques are in operation in the other lines with reference to the foreground. Clearly, the middleground *subdivides* the foreground, while the background *shifts* the foreground.

All the rhythmic detail in the Variations can be traced to these two fundamental techniques, which originate in the Theme's top line. No additional techniques are introduced. What does happen, however, is that these techniques operate at the individual rhythmic levels. (Each level, of course, comprises more than one line in the total texture.) This means that the linear complex at, say, the middleground level alone may exhibit the same type of interaction as occurs between the middleground and background in the Theme's top line.

RHYTHMIC STRUCTURE OF THE VARIATIONS

Example 5 presents a view of the rhythmic structure of the Variations. The same procedures were used here as in the analysis of the Theme. Here too only the top line of the first five-measure phrase is shown, except for Variation III, which, because of the overlapping in the background, requires the entire ten-measure period for complete grouping patterns on all levels.

Rhythmic development within the individual Variations is not adequately represented in Example 5. Most frequently, this development involves the retention and intensification of one or the other of the two rhythmic techniques at a particular level in one or more specific voices. This brings about the periodic predominance of one of the contrapuntal layers, and this often takes the form of various types of hemiola patterns at the foreground level.

Even a brief examination of Example 5 will indicate to what extent the rhythmic potential of the Theme is realized in the Variations. Further study will reveal a manifold of related events, *all of which result from the fundamental duple-triple ordering.*

EXAMPLE 5

THE ROLE OF TEMPO IN THE RHYTHMIC STRUCTURE

It has been shown that the Variations as well as the Theme exhibit a melodic and rhythmic texture that has as its rationale a combination of duple and triple ordering. This ordering can be conceived more comprehensively as a proportionality between all patterns, a proportionality that can be expressed most succinctly as the ratio 2 : 3 (or its inversion, 3 : 2). The complex of relationships that exists between levels is not quite as simple as this, for it is conditioned by the operation of the two fundamental techniques. But the events arising from the operation of these

EXAMPLE 6

techniques can themselves be reduced to duple and triple regroupings. The techniques therefore may be viewed as consequent extensions of the basic proportional relationships that were first given in the Theme.

In view of this controlling proportionality, it becomes apparent that the tempi of the Variations must be selected with care so that there results a correct enunciation of the rhythmic relationships in all spans and all dimensions of the total composition. A survey of the rhythmic texture that results from a correct tempo sequence is given in Example 6. (This example shows only foreground and middleground, i.e., what is most obvious in the notation, since the inclusion of the background would be extremely awkward to present visually.)

In Example 6 the Theme may be considered as a foreground pattern (a series of regularly recurring accents.) The Variations then become a many-voiced middleground pattern that unfolds in relation to the Theme, and the entire texture reveals itself as *an amplified and elaborated duplication of the threefold rhythmic structure of the Theme's top line.* The term duplication used here has more than metaphorical significance; there are a number of specific parallels; e.g., the foreground pattern of Variation IV has the effect of regrouping the Theme's foreground so as to form a texture that is exactly like the texture formed by the middleground and background in the Theme's top line, measures 1–3 (cf. Ex. 3).

SOME SIGNIFICANT EVENTS SHOWN IN EXAMPLE 6

1. The ♪ of Variation I equals 𝅘𝅥𝅯 of the Theme, thus continuing the pattern *but regrouping* (shifting).

2. Variation III shifts the foreground accent of the Theme and further implies a $\frac{6}{8}$-like subdivision of the Theme's basic pulse. This is in contrast to Variation IV, which implies $\frac{2}{4}$ by its regrouping. The middleground patterns in these variations are therefore exact reversals of the metrical orderings, suggesting, in accord with the notion of structural layers, that the metrical patterns are originally derived from the middleground.

3. As it shifts the foreground accent, Variation V subdivides each ♪ of Variation IV into ♪♪♪ . This $\frac{6}{8}$-like pattern is in turn regrouped by the pattern in Variation VIII.

4. Perhaps the most complex regrouping of the Theme's foreground occurs in Variation VII, the only variation slower than the Theme. Other than Variation IV, to which it is closely related, Variation VII is the only

one that shifts the Theme's foreground without simultaneously subdividing it.

PERSISTENCE OF THE BASIC PULSE

Example 7 presents the durational value in each Variation equivalent to the basic metrical unit of the Theme. Each of these values is expressed by a rhythmic figure characteristic to the particular variation. Example 7 is also a partial inventory of important rhythmic figures in the finale—an indication that the finale is literally a summing-up of the entire work.

EXAMPLE 7: DURATIONAL VALUES IN EACH VARIATION THAT ARE EQUIVALENT TO THE BASIC METRICAL UNIT OF THE THEME (M.M. 60)

Variation I	♩‿♪ 𝄾 𝄾 (triplet)	Expressed as prominent rhythmic figure and as 𝄽 𝄾 (triplet)
Variation II	𝅗𝅥	Characteristic rhythmic element in this variation
Variation III	♩.	Expressed as ♪♩ and as ♩♪ throughout
Variation IV	♩	Its equivalent, ♫ is characteristic bass figure
Variation V	♩.	Occurs as ♪♪♪♪♪♪ and as ♩ ♩ ♩ (in hemiola patterns)
Variation VI	♩.	Expressed ♩‿♪ and as ♪♬♪
Variation VII	♩	Occurs as ♪.𝅘𝅥𝅯 and as ♩ (both in hemiola patterns)
Variation VIII	♩.	Comprises an entire measure (♪♪♪♪♪♪)

Variation VII is particularly interesting with regard to the equivalences given in Example 7. In its last section this Variation exploits the durational equivalence of dotted eighth and sixteenth to quarter of the Theme (both equal M.M. 60) in the prolongation, by repetition, of a hemiola until the given meter ($\frac{6}{8}$) is almost completely replaced.

INCOMPLETE MEASURE GROUPINGS OF VARIATIONS IN RELATION TO THEME

It should be remarked that Variations IV and VII have measure groupings that do not end with complete measures at the completion of the first ten-measure period of the Theme. This does not indicate an aproportional relationship (a relationship outside the duple-triple ordering), but only points up the fact that rhythmic interaction within the

Theme is most perceptible and most significant at the middleground rather than at the foreground level. Closer examination reveals that the middleground patterns in the two variations actually *do correspond* with proportional exactitude to the foreground grouping of the Theme. Variation IV unfolds sixteen groups of two while the Theme's twenty pulses are stated. Variation VII is more complicated because of its intricate middleground pattern, but it too ends with a complete group in the middleground.

KEY RHYTHMIC FIGURES

If small (temporal) units or "agents" were discovered which would represent the correct proportional relationships throughout the composition it would be possible to deal more efficiently with the rhythmic complex that has been indicated in Example 6. Such agents do exist. They are called here "key rhythmic figures" both because they give the necessary aural clues to tempo and also because, as significant middleground figures, they are concise expressions of the essential melodic-rhythmic relationships that pervade the entire composition.

Each key rhythmic figure, which is either partially or completely coextensive with the characteristic adjacent tone motive of the Theme's top line, comprises a durational value that is equivalent to either ♩ or ♪ of the Theme. It is apparent that this equivalence makes for ease of perception, particularly with regard to continuity. There follows a complete list of these figures, their equivalent durations in the Theme, and the precise metronome indication for the tempo of each variation (Ex. 8).

Note that when the key rhythmic figure is compared to the adjacent tone figure of the Theme it is either incomplete melodically (it is not a complete adjacent tone figure) or incomplete rhythmically (it does not conform to the stress-release-stress sequence established in the Theme's middleground and foreground). This avoidance of a complete statement of a figure within the composition is comparable to the avoidance of a full cadence or the delay of a full cadence in the overall harmonic framework.

THE KEY RHYTHMIC FIGURE IN RELATION TO THE VARIATIONS' RHYTHMIC STRUCTURE

The key rhythmic figure works with one of the more easily perceptible rhythmic levels (generally foreground or middleground) except in Variations VI and VII. In Variation VI it works with a pattern that shifts

EXAMPLE 8

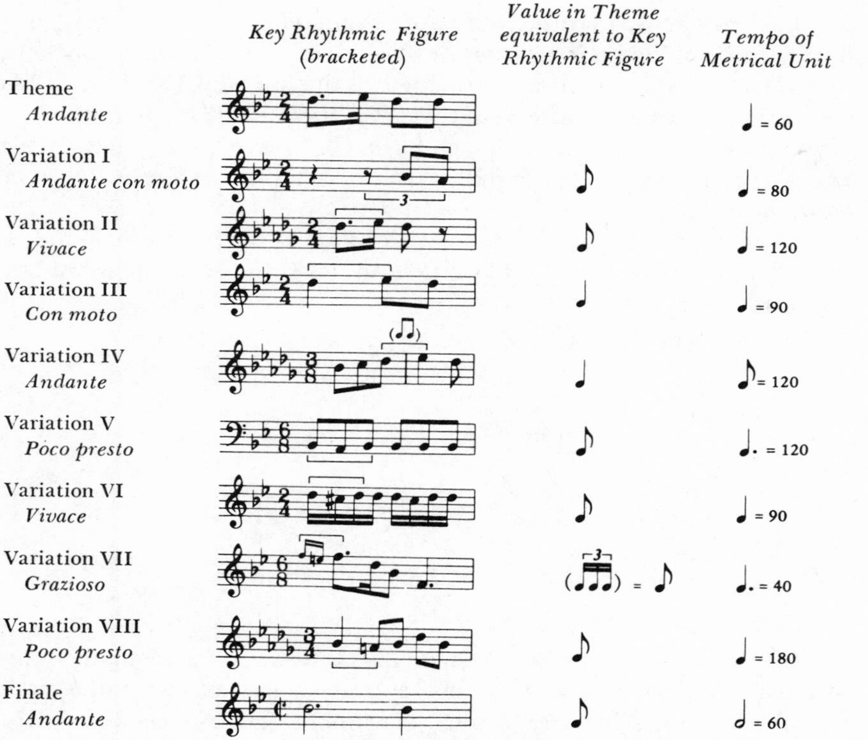

the foreground accent in a way that does not occur in the middleground or background (which are almost identical and are both close to the foreground). The key rhythmic figure in Variation VII is in a similar situation except that the technique in operation there is subdivision.[2] Thus, the key rhythmic figure, because it is so closely identified with the tempo, may be heard to generate an additional rhythmic level, particularly where —as in this case—the other levels correspond so closely.

2. The questions of where the ornament at the beginning of Variation VII falls in relation to the foreground pulse, and how much value it receives, are readily answered if we realize that the adjacent tone figure groups itself most easily and that it requires a stress on the first tone of the group. Thus, the ornament begins on the downbeat and is played in a proportional rhythm. Heard in this way the top line's key rhythmic figure is easily located and Variation VII assumes its correct tempo position. The ornament is omitted from the orchestral version—it would be interesting to find out why. In the two-piano version, when played on the beat in the manner described, it is perfectly simple and clearly perceptible.

TEMPO PROGRESSION

In the larger span of the composition, therefore, tempo is the agency through which rhythmic relationships are correctly articulated, not only with reference to the rhythmic structures of the individual variations, but with reference to the entire work. *Tempo,* then, *is not something to be imposed on the work; it is as integral a part of the rhythmic structure as any of the detailed configurations in the smallest dimension of the composition.*

The tempo progression may be understood as the largest temporal aspect of the foreground. Its cohesiveness and essential relatedness are best expressed as a series of proportions (Ex. 9).

EXAMPLE 9: TEMPO PROGRESSION WITH REFERENCE TO THE THEME

		Ratio to Theme
Variation	I	4 : 3
	II	2 : 1
	III	3 : 2
	IV	2 : 1
	V	2 : 1
	VI	3 : 2
	VII	2 : 3
	VIII	3 : 1

Observe that the ratios given in Example 9 are based upon duple and triple orderings and therefore entirely consistent with the basic melodic-rhythmic structure. In some cases more than one possible tempo would be in accord with the fundamental duple and triple ordering. *But that only one tempo is precisely correct can be quickly demonstrated.* If, for example, Variation II were played at a tempo of ♩ = 100 or ♩ = 140 (in proportions to the Theme of 5 : 3 and 7 : 3, respectively) undesirable equivalences would be brought about between durations in the Variation and durations in the Theme; e.g., the nearest value to 100 in the Theme (where ♩ = 60) is ♪♪ (= approx. 104). Even assuming that a pulse of 104 could be heard as 100, the rhythmic shape is a composite that does not occur on any rhythmic level stated or implied in the Theme. Hence, it is entirely artificial in that it is outside the structural terms of the composition. As for the other tempo possibility, the closest equivalent in the Theme to 140 is ♪♪ (= 144), also a composite that does not occur. At these tempi, therefore, rhythmic relationships between levels would not be clearly perceived even within the individual variations because of the aproportionality arising between non-equivalent values in the Variations and the Theme.

EXAMPLE 10: TEMPO PROGRESSION FROM VARIATION TO VARIATION

	Ratio	
Variation I	4 : 3	Theme
II	3 : 2	Variation I
III	3 : 4	II
IV	4 : 3	III
V	1 : 1	IV
VI	3 : 4	V
VII	4 : 9	VI
VIII	9 : 2	VII
Finale	1 : 3	VIII

Example 10 shows the tempo progression from variation to variation. In contrast to Example 9 there are now three variations that are relatively slower. We also find that the last two ratios are not in accord with the fundamental duple-triple ordering. (The difference between the terms of the proportions is a prime number other than 3.) These ratios simply indicate how the technique of shifting affects relationships between successive variations, relationships which become increasingly complex. These deviant ratios point up the necessity for hearing all of the variations in relation to the Theme in order to avoid hearing the individual variations as isolated compositions.

To sum up, the tempo progression is one of the larger rhythmic patterns in the composition. If translated into a series of conventional note values (Ex. 11) this pattern appears as a composite of types of rhythmic groupings that occur in the Theme and in the Variations. Implicit in the pattern is the basic technique of regrouping. In Example 11 the given values have been subdivided according to a theoretical series of 32nd note sextuplets; the number of these 32nd notes belonging to each value is indicated by the lowest row of numbers. The purpose of this is to illustrate more clearly the internal grouping of the pattern.

EXAMPLE 11: WITH CONTINUOUS REFERENCE TO THE THEME THE TEMPO PROGRESSION IS REPRESENTED AS A SUCCESSION OF RELATIVE NOTE VALUES

	Theme	*I*	*II*	*III*	*IV*	*V*	*VI*	*VII*	*VIII*	*Finale*
Tempo of Basic Unit	60	80	120	90	120	120	90	40	180	60
Succession of Relative Values										
Number of Equivalent  Units	12	9	6	8	6	6	8	18	4	12

THE FINALE

It has been suggested that the finale is literally a summing-up of the entire composition. However, it is more than a kind of reprise. What particularly distinguishes the finale from the Variations is the progressive intensification of the fundamental techniques at the most perceptible middleground level in such a way as to lead to specific points of structural climax. The rhythmic texture becomes progressively complex as it leads through these points, which are followed by phases of less intense activity.

Each change in rhythmic texture is prepared. For example, the group of three eighth notes introduced in m. 25 prepares quite obviously for the eighth note triplet introduced in m. 31. And even before this a similar relationship is to be heard between the grouping of quarter notes at the very beginning and the subsequent introduction of quarter note triplets in m. 15.

The compounding of triplets in mm. 38–45 is the most elaborate manifestation of the technique of subdivision (on an explicitly stated rhythmic pattern), while the displacement of the foreground pattern by the value of ♪ in mm. 56–60 is the fullest application of the shifting technique. This event, which is perhaps the rhythmic climax of the work, is a complete and prolonged regrouping of the foreground, a regrouping that is completely in accord with the rhythmic rationale of the work in its total span. And at the same time this regrouping develops logically and perceptibly from the texture immediately preceding it. In the orchestral version solo oboe is given the figure that prepares the shift (in m. 51). This of course has the effect of making the figure extremely lucid, much more so than in the two-piano version where it is apt to be obscured in the complex of lines.

MELODIC GENESIS OF THE COMPOSITION

There is a further subtlety in the Theme's top line which can now be exposed without the encumbrance of detail: the middleground grouping of the top line transforms the inherent or background pattern so as to engender a passing tone figure in place of the second adjacent tone group (see Ex. 3). This provides a clue to the genesis of the Variations and indeed to the entire composition, for it is the first occurrence of *regrouping,* the basic event from which the two techniques, subdivision and shifting, arise. Furthermore, in the interaction of adjacent tone and passing tone figures, which is an essentially melodic event and not dependent upon any rhythmic attributes of the middleground or foreground level, we see the germination and significance of the duple-triple ordering: the duple ordering of the middleground generates phases of non-completion, or prolongation, whereas the triple ordering of the background generates phases of completion, closure.

SUMMARY

In view of the tempo progression revealed by the analysis, it is clear that the Italian terms are only general directions. That these directions, as compared to the tempi derived from the music itself, are relatively insignificant is pointed up by the fact that the orchestral version of the work bears a different set of terms from the two-piano version. Both sets of terms are given below for comparison.

EXAMPLE 12

Op. 56*a* (Orchestral score published in 1874)	Op. 56*b* (Two-piano score published in 1873)
Theme: *Andante*	Theme: *Andante*
Variation I: *Poco più animato*	Variation I: *Andante con moto*
II: *Più vivace*	II: *Vivace*
III: *Con moto*	III: *Con moto*
IV: *Andante con moto*	IV: *Andante*
V: *Vivace*	V: *Poco presto*
VI: *Vivace*	VI: *Vivace*
VII: *Grazioso*	VII: *Grazioso*
VIII: *Presto non troppo*	VIII: *Poco presto*
Finale: *Andante*	Finale: *Andante*

Observe that only the Theme, Finale and Variations III, VI and VII agree horizontally. This agreement is offset, however, by the inconsistency within each version, particularly the orchestral.

The main result of this analysis will perhaps bear repeating now. It is this:

Rhythmic relationships inherent in the Theme's top line are amplified in a larger span of the total work. In order to articulate these relationships correctly—and indeed the rhythmic structure of the Theme itself—it is essential that the tempi of the Variations be correctly proportional to the tempo of the Theme. Tempo is thus an important aspect of the rhythmic structure—more specifically, an aspect of the foreground structure.

It should be pointed out that the experiencing of this rhythmic complex is dependent solely upon the elementary musical ability to perceive subdivisions of pulses in ordered groups, including partial statements of these groups. Also essential is the ability to grasp and to work with regrouping of all kinds.

MAX KALBECK

[*The Metaphysical Essence of the* Chorale St. Antoni *and Brahms's Variations*]†

Max Kalbeck (1850–1921), the principal biographer of Brahms, first became acquainted with the composer in 1874, but did not begin his comprehensive work until 1897. It is clear that Brahms eventually regarded him as a good friend and member of his circle, though rarely as a confidant. Kalbeck's *métier* of literature and music took him to Vienna in 1880 as a music critic, on Hanslick's recommendation, for the *Wiener Allgemeine Zeitung*. After three years he joined the *Neue freie Presse,* and in 1886 moved to the *Neue Wiener Tageblatt*. Besides his reviews and *feuilletons,* he prepared German translations of operas by Smetana, Leoncavallo, and Mozart. For his friend Johann Strauss the Younger, he was co-author of the book for the Strauss Jubilee operetta, *Jabuka* (1894). Kalbeck was also an avid collector of music autographs and literary works. His enormous collection of Brahmsiana, especially rich in memorabilia, has only in recent years been broken up and dispersed throughout the world.

Kalbeck was an imaginative poet at heart and evidently was attracted to the imagery of grotesque and demonic allegory and metaphor which appealed to German writers and artists—as well as readers—at the turn of the century. How Brahms would have reacted to this essay in allegorical and analytical fantasy, one can only speculate. Sir Donald Tovey was relieved that "Brahms did not live to see this outrage on one of his most serenely beautiful monuments to the joy of sanity"; but within a moment was himself carried away by Kalbeck's power of suggestion and proceeded

† From Max Kalbeck, *Johannes Brahms,* 4 vols. in 8, 3rd ed. (Berlin, Deutsche Brahms-Gesellschaft, 1908–14), II/2, pp. 466–75. Reproduced in translation by kind permission of the copyright owner, Musikverlag Hans Schneider, Tutzing über München. Translation by Margit Lundstrom McCorkle.

to analyze the work with some of Kalbeck's metaphoric tolling bells and dark and mysterious tones intermingled with his own impressionistic metaphors (*Essays in Musical Analysis* [London, 1935], II, pp. 136–39). Robert Haven Schauffler was more indignant: "Kalbeck['s] weakest point was his desire to embellish absolute music with far-fetched literary programs . . . Programmatists have seldom fallen to lower depths of absurdity than this" (*The Unknown Brahms* [New York, 1933], p. 417).

Here follows what is probably the first publication in an English translation. The essay has been abridged by elimination of several superfluous footnotes and musical examples.

[1]

The inscription of the Andante [*Chorale St. Antoni*], obviously a citation, had some significance and pointed the powerfully stimulated imagination of the composer in a definite direction. Like a religious procession with fluttering banners, the half-solemn, half-merry theme was in motion amid ringing bells. By means of an arbitrary rhythmic augmentation or doubling of the second beat, the march always came to a standstill at a certain place and then had to be put into a brisk trot again; a realistic tone picture, taken from life! To what chapel did the splendid pilgrimage go? To the honor of which Antonius did its song resound? Deep in the core the melody, endowed with a sensual-spiritual doubleface, burned with holy life; and out from the mysterious center, dazzling shafts of light, which illuminated the most adventurous tone pictures, burst forth toward all sides. These concurred with impressions of religious genre-painting, which Brahms had received from pictures of older and more recent times. In his imagination a mystical miracle took place: he became a witness to the temptations to which the holy Antonius of Thebes was exposed a thousand or more years ago as he let his body burn in the desert. The musician also felt the stigmata on his own skin, as the poet Gustave Flaubert [1821–80] and the painter Anselm Feuerbach [1829–80] had felt them; but he did not risk his life the same as they had, but left it to the imagination of the listeners to make what they would out of the variations on the *Chorale St. Antoni*.

In his notes Feuerbach informs [us] about a life-size painting, *Temptation of Saint Anthony*, from [his] Karlsruhe period [1854–55]:

> The picture had a vertical format [showing a] wooded interior with life-size trees. A Dominican monk knelt below with hands pressed to his breast; whip, book, and skull lay nearby. In the background, dark against the evening sky and the landscape, stood a female form who appeared to

> call to him to enter into the real life in the place of senseless devotion. That was the approximate idea.[1]

In the first rage over the stupidity with which the picture was reviewed at its first public exhibition, the artist destroyed it. But Allgeyer in Munich prepared a beautiful reproduction of the painting from an old daguerreotype which still existed. Allgeyer also had a photographic exposure made from an oil sketch of Feuerbach's, treating the same subject, which had found its way to Augsburg.[2]

> It is exactly the same female form in altogether the same alluring posture; only she does not stand here as there, with the full weight of earthly gravity on the ground, but on the contrary, she has become a hovering, lust-bearing vision. Surrounded by a cloud halo, in motion up and down, playing and making music among the charming cherubs, she seems to have called the music to help as a newly enticing power in the service of seduction. The Saint has buried his countenance in his arms, thrown himself to earth as if to the last protection from the overpowering of the sense-ensnaring spell. At the critical moment, the artist now has three of the great church fathers of mighty stature come forward for the restoration of the ethical equilibrium. They call out to the despairing one to persevere in the battle against sin and hell's deception, while on their signal the monk's books, as the sources of frivolous human knowledge, burst high into flames.[3]

Here we have a range of ideas which is in accord with the emotional content of the Brahms composition and [we] also find the direct allusion to the music; the painter came to realize that he alone could not master the subject, and summoned the allied arts to help. That Flaubert and Brahms occupied themselves simultaneously with the same subject—*La tentation de Saint Antoine* was published in the same year as the orchestral variations (1874)—is an interesting coincidence and an additional argument for the fact that a telepathic communication exists between productive geniuses. But the concord [of Brahms] with Feuerbach and the fact that the musician picked up the thread again where it had broken away from the painter, reveal a conscious purpose and make it highly probable that Brahms, in the composition of his work, had thought

1. Paraphrased by Kalbeck from Feuerbach's own description. See *Ein Vermächtnis von Anselm Feuerbach,* ed. Henriette Feuerbach, 2nd ed. (Vienna, 1885); new edition with introduction by Marianne Fleischhack (Berlin, n.d.). [*Editor*]

2. Both photographic copies are reproduced in Herman Uhde-Bernays, ed., *Feuerbach. Des Meisters Gemälde in 200 Abbildungen.* (*Klassiker der Kunst in Gesamtausgaben,* 23 [Stuttgart & Berlin, 1913]), pp. 52–53; and in H. Bodmer, *Feuerbach* (Leipzig, 1942), pp. 23–24. [*Editor*]

3. Quoted by Kalbeck from Julius Allgeyer, *Anselm Feuerbach; Sein Leben und seine Kunst* (Bamberg, 1894); 2nd ed., Berlin & Stuttgart, 1904). [*Editor*]

of the unfortunate desert Saint of his friend and further beyond him to the holy Antonius himself.[4]

Whether or not the Saint of the pilgrim song [*Wallfahrerlied*] scored by Haydn is Antonius of Padua, which certainly could easily be, is not of further importance to us. As the hero of the Brahms variations-symphony, we honor Antonius the Great, the steadfast royal scion of Heraclea, who renounced his title, bestowed his goods on the poor, marched naked into the desert, and lived on roots and leaves, the combatant and victor who subdued in his own body all devils and demons and the chief of the devils.[5] Cross, skull, and whip are his household furniture, but also the beautiful woman, the bell, and the songbook, his

4. The author [Kalbeck] remembers a conversation that he had with Brahms at the beginning of the eighties. We turned to the point that the Catholic Church has always known how to, and never disdained to, work on the senses of the faithful, often with the grossest means of all. We happened to speak of the legends of the saints and their relationship to pictorial art. I referred to the contradiction of which the old Netherlandish genre painters *a la* [David] Teniers [1582–1649] in particular have come to be guilty, in the innumerably repeated representation of the subject of the temptation of the holy Antonius, in that amongst loudly forbidding, horribly ridiculous monsters they hung around the neck of the Saint a slightly desirable woman, who must have appeared doubly suspicious owing to the furious uproar of his surroundings. This only gives evidence of the naïveté and pious disposition of those painters, opined Brahms, and would be entirely to the taste of the Church; for sensual pleasure mingled with horror would make a far stronger impression on simple souls than chaste beauty. And how ought the painter to indicate that the vision of the young woman who offers a cup of wine to the anchorite is of the devil, if he did not also have a goblin riding on a broomstick? "One [painter] attempted to treat the story without magic contrivances: Feuerbach. Consequently, he has transformed the ancient holy Antonius into a modern monk, and his attempt was ill rewarded. Do you know the picture?" He [Brahms] fetched the photograph from his Feuerbach portfolio and made me a present of it along with other reproductions from Feuerbach, since he was pleased to discover in me an admirer of the painter. "After all," he continued hesitantly and a little self-consciously or uncertainly, "the whole thing is no business for paintings. Poets and musicians could make a profit from it sooner" [*Ubrigens . . . ist das Ganze kein Geschäft für die Malerei. Dichter und Musiker könnten eher davon profitieren*]. He looked at me sideways while he was saying this, as if he expected from me a certain remark. I did not understand his meaning then, but believed that he wanted to know something about Flaubert, with whom he was not familiar.

5. St. Antonius the Great, or St. Anthony of Egypt (250–356 A.D.), as distinguished from the more popular St. Antonius, or St. Anthony, of Padua (1195–1231), was the founder of monasticism and thus had an enormous influence in early Christendom. A hermit, he endured the legendary temptations in the desert. St. Anthony of Padua, a Franciscan, was an advocate of St. Augustine's theology and an influential preacher against heresy. As the apostle of charity, his intercession is sought by the faithful in everyday matters of health and happiness. His feast day is June 13. Thus, the so-called *Chorale St. Antoni* allegedly honors St. Anthony of Padua, while the Brahms variations, in Kalbeck's view, represent the tribulations of St. Anthony the Great. The Feuerbach paintings would presumably also be a composite conception of the ancient temptations occurring to a more modern monk. [*Editor*]

attributes. Before he learned the omnipotent formula of renunciation, the cabalistic incantation with which he banished evil forever, he had to fight out many severe conflicts. Because the foe settled further into the last meager sweetness of his lonely life and plagued the poor soul of the hermit who relied on book and bell. Whenever he opened the book, alluring mirages of imagination rose out of the song lines along with the pious sounds, and they interwove themselves with the latter into a round dance of enticing forms, which provokingly encircled the fevered head of the penitent, fainting before the cross. It was to no avail that he flagellated himself bloody in order to mortify the desire of his senses, because the blood dripping from his whip was transformed into fragrant roses. And whenever he, benumbed and nearly overwhelmed by the delusive insinuations of the tempter, fearfully rang the little prayer bell, then the silvery distantly audible clang sounded, free of all sorts of nearby rabble, and the echo of the hazy, fabled blue distance promised to restore to him what he had dreamed away and lost of the good things of earth.

[II]

Confronting the Brahms variations at the beginning, we can look over the course of their development, which matches the spiritual proceedings of the human warrior to the glorious conclusion prepared by the divine conqueror. From the graceful first variation to the grandiose finale, the musical-psychological course of the work moves in an ascending line. Only the eighth and last variation, a lugubrious *Presto non troppo* creeping along softly in the dark, submerges the theme in the depths of a ghastly abyss, as it were. But over the grave of earthly joy leads the slim, always broadening route to the summit: its dark threshold is the necessary transition step to the acquired bliss, which is attained with the consummate triumph of the *Chorale St. Antoni,* exalted as a banner carried victoriously throughout all dangers and oppositions.

We have called the work a Symphony in Variations and would only say therewith that its conception aspires to the highest instrumental form. An analogy to the external scheme of the symphony cannot be made even if one were of the mind to combine several variations for a movement. The characteristics of *Scherzo* and *Adagio* are represented in Nos. V and VII [respectively], [and the] beginning and ending correspond with one another as *Allegro* and *Finale.* But the composer does not budge an inch from the form of the theme, a regular, repeated two-part period with coda; he even respects the fundamental harmonic relationships of the theme, permitting the key of B♭-major to alternate three times with B♭-minor, [and] the duple [meter to alternate] four times with the triple meter.

As the first variation proceeds directly out of the theme, so one variation seems to develop out of the other—musical *dissolving views*.[6] The sound of bells fading away in the song is picked up and, [used] as a motive, combined with counterpoint. With the first of five bell chimes which are intoned in the orchestra by the wind instruments, the demons hurry hither from afar; they come on the chords of the string quartet in order to assemble in the vicinity with the spirits ascending from the *Chorale*. Both swarm around, a host of airy skirmishers, and open the battle as the advance post of the devil. Each part can exchange places with the other, each performs as if it sang in its own fashion until the other is pleased to assimilate it, and together all form the concerto which in the breast of *Saint Anthony* surges and struggles to objectify itself externally. If the theme has determined the plan and design for the construction of the whole, then the introductory first variation may already be recognized as [the] propelling principal power of the motion and development of the double counterpoint. Aesthetic worth and logical conformity of the musico-theoretical means produced by bunglers in ill-repute are hardly to be convincingly demonstrated as with this finest of musical images created by [the] master hand. Through the management of the voices alone more variety is produced in the work than through choice and combination of instruments, although concerning the color magnificence and the luster of the instrumental effects, precisely here too Brahms is in no way inferior to the greatest orchestral painter.

Each variation has its special color which again is differentiated in countless gradations. One might compare the three variations in minor, Nos. II, IV, and VIII, with one another in order to see what difference of character has been imprinted upon them by their instrumentation despite their tonality and mood relationship!

[The] *forte* strokes of the full orchestra, which always cause the bell motive to sound together with the three first notes of the theme, alternate with a soft, sad round-dance melody produced by the woodwinds and accompanied by muted *pizzicatos* (Var. II). Oboe and horn begin to sing in octaves a sweet and simple dirge surrounded by slurred sixteenths

6. Kalbeck uses the English term "dissolving views" in allusion to the photographic technique current in his time, in which a picture projected by a "magic" lantern was caused to dissolve gradually into the next picture without abrupt transition. [*Editor*]

from the viola, and deliver it in double counterpoint at the twelfth to the strings; while flutes, oboes, and bassoons [*recte* flute, clarinet, bassoon] take possession of the sixteenth-note figure, which now steps forward as the superior melody (Var. IV). Muted violas and cellos begin a figured melody, sinister as fog brewing over chasmal depths, wandering away in the dark, always *pianissimo*. Out of the upper register, where the former are answered in the inversion by the woodwinds, the piccolo becomes a pale, piercing light on the whitish-gray fermenting substance; it disperses itself, and one imagines looking into an open grave (Var. VIII). With what hopeless and desolate spiritual torment the shocked eyewitness to the dismal scene gazes down into the abyss which devoured his beloved, the heart-rending passage [see mm. 342–46f] makes manifest.

No less numerous and characteristic are the orchestral effects which cause the variations in major to perform in the most diverse colors. In the third [variation], especially richly elaborated, oboes and bassoons sing tender duets alternately with the strings; flutes and bassoons wreathe the lovely melody with dainty flower garlands, and in between, horns call portentously. In the six-eight meter of the fifth variation a swarm of roguish, insect-like sprites amuse themselves [as] illustrated by woodwinds and strings. Their restless eighth-note figures, whirring around *piano* and *staccato*, set in motion all kinds of piquant rhythmic mischief, push suddenly vigorously against simple time divisions, smuggle in the three-four meter, become overloud and undersoft, and turn the lowest to the highest. It is said of the devils of the holy Antonius that they sometimes built their nest within him like the smallest parasite, sometimes frightened him by colossal size. Gigantically they roar in the *Vivace* of the sixth variation. The piece sounds like the breakthrough of the wild chase; the four horns call forth from the clouds, in which it is lightening and thundering, a mounted band of superhuman forms. By this time in the score one sees the fiery serpents as it were following an up-and-down, zigzag course, and when one hears them, the strange keys (G-flat major and B-flat minor, C-flat major and E-flat minor) thus strengthen the dazzling impression of their precipitous bursting into flames. Antonius is lifted up in the air by the demons and dashed to earth, as the [Martin] Schongauer engraving shows it.[7]

7. Schongauer (ca. 1450–91), the great German painter and engraver, produced an engraving, *Tribulations of Saint Anthony,* which was extraordinarily influential during the late 15th- and early 16th-centuries, and especially on Dürer. In it the grotesque, unearthly demons, nine in a circle, are beating and tearing at the Saint in mid-air. The engraving is reproduced in H. W. Janson and Joseph Kerman, *A History of Art*

But the most difficult test awaits the saint in the seventh variation; it is the cruelest because it is at the same time the sweetest. "Vanish, you dark vaults above," the invisible spirits appear to sing. A bewitching siciliano—whose solo is intoned at first by flutes and violas, while a choir of winds and violins accompanies in a moderately descending scalar middle voice, and the basses play a tender melody in countermotion to it—casts a spell before our senses over the most splendid feminine image from among others like her, perchance a Leda who awaits her swan. The register of the voices changes already as a consequent of the first part, the same performance being repeated under altered conditions; painful, incisive, momentarily suspended notes, which serve to the further intensification of the divine desire, cause the song to swell ever more passionately. All instruments are participating in it at last; syncopations and rhythmic displacements would desire to endow the fleeting rapture with permanence, horn and violins [would] detain them with heartfelt supplication. Everything earlier seems only to have been preparation for this wonderful piece, which can compete with the loveliest presentations of music, even with the Shepherds' Symphony in Bach's *Christmas Oratorio,* which it calls to mind from afar. A passage such as [mm. 311–15f.] is not forgotten again when once it has been heard; it sounds like the embodiment of all sweet secrecy, like the quintessence of the bliss of all living creatures, which, according to Meister Eckhart [von Hochheim (1260?–1328?)], is "mixed with bitterness." After it comes death.

Blessed the man who has withstood the test! He is celebrated by the finale, which includes seventeen or more variations in one. They are erected over an ever so oft repeated basso ostinato [see mm. 361–66], and this bass, obtained by the rhythmic modification of the main theme [see mm. 1–3], brings back finally in triumph, after magnificent climaxes [of a] thematic, instrumental, and dynamic nature, the *Chorale St. Antoni,* as if the most supreme commander of the heavenly troops had had it thrown into the midst of the hostile tumult of the assaulting sons of hell in order that it would be dragged out by his Saint.

---

and Music (Englewood Cliffs, [1968]), and in C. I. Minott, *Martin Schongauer* (New York, [ca. 1971]). [*Editor*]

VIEWS AND COMMENTS

EDUARD HANSLICK

[*Review of the First Performance of Op. 56a*]†

Eduard Hanslick (1825–1904), the preeminent music critic, had long before established his international reputation as a discerning and courageous music journalist. His philosophy of musical aesthetics, as set forth in 1854 in his book *Vom Musikalisch-Schönen* (The Beautiful in Music), maintaining that "ideas which a composer expresses are mainly and primarily of a purely musical nature," was tremendously influential throughout the century. It inevitably brought him into hostility with Wagner and the "Music of the Future," but conversely made him the foremost exponent of the classical tradition. He was one of Brahms's closest friends, as well as champion, during the composer's thirty-seven years in Vienna, and was honored with the dedication of the *Waltzes,* Op. 39.

In his review of the first performance of the *Haydn Variations* by members of the Vienna Court Opera Orchestra in the opening Philharmonic concert of 1873 (November 2), with Brahms conducting, Hanslick was enthusiastic, though typically cautious in assessing a new work on first hearing.

For the first time we have heard a new orchestral work by Brahms: "Theme with Variations" (Op. 56).[1] Brahms seems to us now like a robust tree standing in full sap, whose green branches are stretching ever higher and wider, bearing ever more abundant, sweeter fruits.[2] It is a joy to

† From the review published in *Die Neue freie Presse;* republished in Eduard Hanslick, *Concerte, Componisten und Virtuosen der letzten fünfzehn Jahre; 1870–1885* (Berlin, 4th ed., 1896), pp. 71–72. Translation by Margit Lundstrom McCorkle.

1. The *Haydn Variations* was the first orchestral work by Brahms to have a premiere in Vienna, and the second of his works to be performed by the Philharmonic. [*Editor*]

2. Hanslick was fond of metaphors related to nature, which are sometimes difficult to translate while conveying the meaning he probably intended. This particular botanical metaphor in the original German reads as follows: "Brahms erscheint uns jetzt wie ein kräftiger, in vollem Safte stehender Baum, der seine grünen Äste immer höher und weiter streckt, immer reichlichere, süssere Früchte trägt." [*Editor*]

watch this healthy productive force. Each success achieved makes him at the same time more severe toward himself and more generous toward the world. In earnest, not irksome labor, in the full joyousness of creating, Brahms brings us now with each autumn a richer harvest.

The theme of the variations (Andante, B♭ major, $\frac{2}{4}$) was probably originally a pilgrimage song (*Wallfahrtslied*) of popular, pious expression, simple and yet very singular owing to its five-measure rhythm. Brahms has scored it very simply and beautifully, merely winds and basses;[3] the violins [and violas] join in initially with figuration in the first variation. We would gladly have characterized these variations in detail (there are eight and a finale), if only to show the reader how skillfully through the alternation between major and minor [and] through diversity of tempo, meter, and instrumentation Brahms prevents monotony and yet combines the parts into an organic unity. But such a word description is too idle and dismal a thing in the face of a genuine, instrumentally conceived composition.

The serious, almost pious expression of the whole, as well as the polyphonic and contrapuntal mastery repeatedly calls to mind Sebastian Bach; yet nowhere does this element push itself forward, constituting, as it were, only the solid, deep foundation over which the silver stream of spontaneous, modern feelings and figures are in motion. The work has the double merit of being not too long and of becoming intensified ever more effectively and spiritedly during its course. If both the first [and second] variations sound to the unprepared listener somewhat dry and not entirely lucid in their figuration, then from the third variation on, an always more independent, individual life flourishes and reaches a captivating climax in the finale. An exuberant, truly musically formative force which does not need to lean on a printed or secret program, here unpretentiously spreads out its treasures. The seriousness and the judicious moderation are strikingly reconciled by Brahms with entirely new, even daring features. An example from the instrumentation: if one were to announce a prize for the composer who introduces piccolo and triangle in such a serious, almost religiously tinged musical composition, without thereby becoming in the least banal or coquettish—who else would probably have the prospect of winning it? Brahms has been able to do this and has used both these unlikely instruments in his variations with the most beautiful effect, so harmoniously and full of character, that one

3. Hanslick meant cellos as well as double basses, of course. The bassoons and contrabassoon were included with the winds. [*Editor*]

cannot imagine at all doing away with them. He furthermore uses with splendid effect the contrabassoon, this venerable instrument [which is] becoming so rare! It gives the whole composition, particularly the theme, an altogether unusual, mysterious, solemn coloring, on account of which we gladly dispense with the pealing luster of the trombones.

HANS GÁL

[*Brahms and His Art of Variation*]†

While still young, Brahms carried on intensive studies along these lines [i.e., the techniques of variation]. His crowning achievements within the scope of piano music are the *Handel* and the *Paganini Variations*. Both deal with the problem of using a theme in a small binary song form, resulting in a procession of numerous short episodes. Beethoven, in his C minor Variations and his Variations in E-flat major (*Eroica*), Opus 35, has shown how this problem can be resolved through linking together two or three consecutive variations by a common, unifying idea and thereby freely organizing a large number of variations into contrasting groups. Brahms successfully attempted the same in his *Handel* and his *Paganini Variations*. In this manner the variation form offers the best and most stimulating possibility for clustering a number of shorter structures into a coherent whole. In his *Variations on a Theme of Haydn*, for orchestra, Brahms followed a different procedure which is frequently found in variations by Beethoven and also in Bach's *Goldberg Variations*, which Brahms loved and studied diligently. In this kind of variations the theme is a larger, self-contained structure, and each variation develops from it as a finished, independently fashioned character piece, so that the series of variations gives an impression rather like that of a suite.

† From Hans Gál, *Johannes Brahms; His Work and Personality*, tr. Joseph Stein. New York, 1963, pp. 171–73, 175 (excerpted). Copyright © 1963 by Alfred A. Knopf, Inc. Reprinted by permission of the publisher.

Consequently the succession of variations is dominated above all by the principle of contrast with its changeable tempi and varying meters.

Brahms also learned from Beethoven how to deal with the problem of the variation finale, whose function is to bring a long series of short pieces to a dynamically summarizing, broadly conceived finish. Like Beethoven, he made use of a large variety of form possibilities. In the *Paganini Variations* it is a greatly enlarged final variation which repeatedly uses the thematic model, and in the *Handel Variations* it is a fugue. In the *Haydn Variations* it is a passacaglia on a five-measure bass motif which, based on the theme itself, finally brings it to a triumphant apotheosis.

In one respect, however, Brahms certainly could not take a joke, though what Wagner had in mind when he made his malicious remark was hardly a joke:[1] the integrity of the theme as a model of form was as sacred to Brahms as it was to Beethoven. However wonderfully his inventions may grow beyond the theme, its basic structure remains unchanged. In a newspaper column Hanslick once quipped about Brahms, who had sprouted a beard during his summer vacation, saying that his original face was just as hard to recognize as the theme in many of his variations. This accusation must have been made many times, but it is really unjustified. It is true that hearing the theme within a variation requires a concentration of musical memory hardly within the capacity of every listener, but such a capacity is not really necessary for the enjoyment of music whose logical coherence is convincing, even if one is not actually conscious of the circumstances underlying this conviction. . . .

* * *

At this stage of his development[2] the variation technique had become an intrinsic part of Brahms's style, just as motivic development had in the case of Beethoven. Since Beethoven's time the variation principle

1. The allusion here is to the comment Wagner is alleged to have made to Brahms following their first meeting, when Brahms played his *Handel Variations* for him. Wagner reputedly remarked to the effect that "One sees what can still be done with the old forms in the hands of one who knows how to deal with them." (Quoted by Karl Geiringer, *Brahms; His Life and Work* [Garden City, 1961], p. 76.) Later, in *On Conducting,* he elaborated on his estimation: "Objectively regarded, there is nothing wrong with these musicians, most of whom compose fairly well. Mr. Johannes Brahms once was good enough to play some pieces with serious variations for me, from which I could tell that he is not a joker, and which I considered quite acceptable." (Quoted by Gál, *op. cit.,* pp. 134–35.) [*Editor*]

2. The author is referring to a later period than the *Haydn Variations,* specifically to that of the *Fourth Symphony,* but the statement is equally relevant to 1873. [*Editor*]

has moved into the realm of the grand form; its possibilities embrace the entire gamut from brief, two-bar ostinato phrases in codas . . . to the imaginative transmutation of themes in the same composer's late sonatas and quartets. With Brahms the variation form penetrated everywhere—into his sonatas, into his rondos, and even into his dance-like intermezzi.

JOHANNES BRAHMS

[*Thoughts on Composing*]

There is no real *creating* . . . without hard work. That which you would call invention, that is to say, a thought, an idea, is simply an inspiration from above, for which I am not responsible, which is no merit of mine. Yea, it is a present, a gift, which I ought even to despise until I have made it my own by right of hard work. And there need be no hurry about that, either. It is as with the seed-corn; it germinates unconsciously and in spite of ourselves. When I, for instance, have found the first phrase of a song . . . I might shut the book there and then, go for a walk, do some other work, and perhaps not think of it again for months. Nothing, however, is lost. If afterward I approach the subject again, it is sure to have taken shape; I can now begin to really work at it. But there are composers who sit at the piano with a poem before them, putting music to it from A to Z until it is done. They write themselves into a state of enthusiasm which makes them see something finished, something important, in every bar.[1]

* * *

One ought never to forget that by actually perfecting *one* piece one gains and learns more than by commencing or half-finishing a dozen. Let

1. From a conversation with George Henschel, February 27, 1876. George Henschel, *Personal Recollections of Johannes Brahms* (Boston, 1907), pp. 22–23.

it rest, let it rest, and keep going back to it and working it over and over again, until it is completed as a finished work of art, until there is not a note too much or too little, not a bar you could improve upon. Whether it is *beautiful* also, is an entirely different matter, but perfect it *must* be. You see, I am rather lazy, but I never cool down over a work, once begun, until it is perfected, unassailable.[2]

* * *

I could wish people would distinguish variations from *fantasia-variations,* or whatever we may choose to call the greater number of modern writings in this form. I have a peculiar affection for the variation form, and consider that it offers great scope to our talents and energies.[3]

* * *

I think here [*Ein deutsches Requiem*] as well as with all other music the metronome is of no value. As far at least as my experience goes, everybody has, sooner or later, withdrawn his metronome marks. Those which can be found in my works—good friends have talked me into putting them there, for I myself have never believed that my blood and a mechanical instrument go well together. The so-called "elastic" tempo is moreover not a new invention. *"Con discrezione"* should be added to that as to many other things. Is this an answer? I know of no better one; but what I do know is that I indicate (without figures) my tempi, modestly, to be sure, but with the greatest care of clearness.[4]

* * *

[With respect to arrangements] I myself, however, prefer to retain my ears and know what is a pianoforte piece and what is an orchestral piece. . . .[5]

2. From a conversation with Henschel, July 13, 1876; *ibid.,* p. 39.

3. From a letter to Heinrich and Elisabet von Herzogenberg, August 20, 1876. *Johannes Brahms; The Herzogenberg Correspondence,* ed. Max Kalbeck, tr. Hannah Bryant (London, 1909), p. 7.

4. From a letter to Henschel, February 1880; *op. cit.,* pp. 78–79.

5. From a letter to Henschel, who had recently become conductor of the new Boston Symphony Orchestra, 1881; *ibid.,* pp. 80–81.

PHILIPP SPITTA

[On the Significance of Brahms]†

The musical politicians of our day call Brahms a reactionary. . . . Others say that Brahms demonstrates practically that in these [i.e., the Classical] forms something new can *still* be said.[1] Not *still,* but always—so long as our music remains, this will be the situation. For these forms are derived from the very inner nature of this music, and in their outlines could not have been more perfectly conceived. Even those composers who think they have broken them, and thereby have accomplished an act of liberation, avail themselves of these forms in so far as they still have any desire at all to achieve a satisfying impression. They cannot do otherwise, so long as composition and contrast in music remain. They only do it much worse than does he who enters into the inheritance from the past with full awareness and with the intention of employing it in the service of the beautiful. Power, of course, is required; moreover, many ways lead to the shrine. Weber and Schubert, Schumann and Gade have in many ways loosened Beethoven's firm construction and are, in the matter of musical architectonics, unquestionably lesser masters. They seek to make up for this deficiency through other, magnificent characteristics; and no one to whom music is more than a mere sort of arithmetic will be so pedantic as to look askance at their weaknesses. But the assumption that their willfulnesses are the guideposts to new and higher goals is false. The foundations must remain fixed, and each one builds upon them ac-

† From Spitta's *Zur Musik,* 16th essay (Berlin, 1892, p. 416 ff). Abridged and quoted by Alfred Einstein, *Music in the Romantic Era,* New York, 1947, p. 153. Reprinted by permission of W. W. Norton & Co., Inc. and J. M. Dent & Sons, Ltd.

1. Obviously, a jibe at Wagner's reputed comment to Brahms after hearing the *Handel Variations* for the first time (see p. 214, n. 1). Spitta's lengthy original statement, however, speaks of "the most capacious (*weitesten*) symphonic forms," which Professor Einstein has abbreviated and freely interpreted in a word as "Classical" forms. [*Editor*]

cording to his needs. After Brahms, others will come who will compose in ways other than his. His endeavor was towards concentration and indissolubly firm union, using all the means that are proper to the art of music as such.

Bibliography

BRAHMS'S LIFE AND WORK

Adler, Guido. "Johannes Brahms; His Achievement, His Personality, and His Position," tr. W. Oliver Strunk, *The Musical Quarterly,* XIX/2 (1933), 113–42. [A brilliant summary of the essence of Brahms by the founder of the Viennese school of musicology.]

Ehrmann, Alfred von. *Johannes Brahms; Weg, Werk und Welt.* Leipzig, 1933. [A useful one-volume biography by an Austrian journalist, poet, and amateur musician.]

Gál, Hans. *Johannes Brahms, His Work and Personality.* Tr. Joseph Stein. New York, 1963. [An interesting survey of certain aspects of Brahms's life and career by the composer who actually prepared the bulk of the *Sämtliche Werke* edition under Mandyczewski's direction.]

Geiringer, Karl. *Brahms; His Life and Work.* Tr. H. B. Weiner and Bernard Miall. Boston and New York, 1936. 2nd ed., Garden City, 1961. [This remains the best biographical and historical survey in English, drawing upon the author's knowledge acquired while curator of the archives of the Gesellschaft der Musikfreunde, Vienna (1930–38).]

Henschel, George. *Personal Recollections of Johannes Brahms.* Boston, 1907.

Heuberger, Richard. *Erinnerungen an Johannes Brahms.* Ed. Kurt Hofmann. Tutzing, 1971.

Kalbeck, Max. *Johannes Brahms.* 4 vols. in 8. 3rd ed. Berlin, 1908–14. [The comprehensive biography of the composer on which all later studies are based.]

May, Florence. *The Life of Johannes Brahms.* 2 vols. London, 1905. 2nd ed., London, [1948?]. [The first biography in English and still valuable.]

Niemann, Walter. *Brahms.* Berlin, 1920. English ed., tr. Catherine Alison Phillips. New York, 1929; repr. New York, 1969.

Schauffler, Robert Haven. *The Unknown Brahms.* New York, 1940; repr. Westport, Conn., [1972]. [An eccentric biography by a facile writer and amateur scholar, but having considerable merit nonetheless because of some information not otherwise available in English.]

CORRESPONDENCE

Brahms, Johannes. *Johannes Brahms Briefwechsel.* 16 vols. Ed. Max Kalbeck, Wilhelm Altmann, Heinrich Barth, Andreas Moser, Leopold Schmidt, Julius Röntgen, Ernst Wolff, Carl Krebs. Berlin, 1908–22; repr. Tutzing, 1974.

——— *und Julius Allgeyer; Eine Künstlerfreundschaft in Briefen.* Ed. Alfred Orel. Tutzing, 1964.

——— *Billroth im Briefwechsel mit Brahms.* [Ed. Otto Gottlieb-Billroth]. Munich & Berlin, 1964.

——— *and Theodor Billroth: Letters from a Musical Friendship.* Tr. and ed. Hans Barkan. Norman, Oklahoma, 1957. [A translation of *Billroth im Briefwechsel mit Brahms.*]

——— *in seiner Familie. Der Briefwechsel.* Ed. Kurt Stephenson. Veröffentlichungen aus der Hamburger Staats- und Universitätsbibliothek, 9. Hamburg, 1973.

——— *Briefe der Freundschaft. Johannes Brahms-Klaus Groth.* Ed. Volquart Pauls. Heide, 1956.

——— *im Briefwechsel mit Eusebius Mandyczewski.* Ed. Karl Geiringer. Leipzig, 1933.

——— *Clara Schumann–Johannes Brahms Briefe aus den Jahren 1853–1896.* Ed. Berthold Litzmann. 2 vols. Leipzig, 1927.

——— *Letters of Clara Schumann and Johannes Brahms, 1853–1896.* Ed. Berthold Litzmann. 2 vols. London, 1927; repr. New York, 1973.

——— *und Fritz Simrock; Weg einer Freundschaft. Briefe des Verlegers an den Komponisten.* Ed. Kurt Stephenson. Veröffentlichungen aus der Hamburger Staats- und Universitätsbibliothek, 6. Hamburg, 1961.

——— *an Julius Spengel. Unveröffentliche Briefe aus den Jahren 1882–1897.* Ed. Annemari Spengel. Hamburg, 1959.

THE MUSIC

Johannes Brahms Sämtliche Werke. Ausgabe der Gesellschaft der Musikfreunde in Wien. 26 vols. [Ed. Eusebius Mandyczewski and Hans Gál]. Leipzig, 1926–28; repr. Ann Arbor, 1949; reissued, Wiesbaden, 1964. [The definitive editions of the Collected Works.]

——— *Thematisches Verzeichniss sämmtlicher im Druck erschienenen Werke von Johannes Brahms. Nebst systematischem Verzeichniss und Registern.* Berlin, 1897, 1902, 1903, 1904, 1910. The 1897 issue reprinted as *The N. Simrock Thematic Catalog of the Works of Johannes Brahms.* New introduction, including addenda and corrigenda, by Donald M. McCorkle. New York, 1973.

——— *Thematisches Verzeichnis seiner Werke.* Ed. Alfred von Ehrmann. Leipzig, 1933. *Anhang: Ergänzungen und Berichtigungen. Idem.*, 1952.

SPECIAL STUDIES, WITH REFERENCE TO BRAHMS'S VARIATIONS AND CREATIVE PROCESS

Blume, Walter, ed. *Brahms in der Meininger Tradition. Seine Sinfonien und Haydn Variationen in der Bezeichnung von Fritz Steinbach.* Stuttgart, [1933]. [Contains phrasing indications of Fritz Steinbach for his interpretation of the Variations for Orchestra. Steinbach (1855–1916) was an important Brahms specialist and on Brahms's recommendation succeeded Hans von Bülow as conductor of the Meiningen Court Orchestra.]

Fellinger, Imogen. *Über die Dynamik in der Musik von Johannes Brahms.* Berlin & Wunsiedel, 1961. [A doctoral dissertation; contains an interesting analysis of the dynamics in the *Haydn Variations.*]

Jonas, Oswald. "Die 'Variationen für eine liebe Freundin' von Johannes Brahms," *Archiv für Musikwissenschaft,* XII/4 (1955), 319–26. [A study of the Library of Congress autograph of the *Handel Variations.*]

Knorr, Iwan. "Johannes Brahms Variationen über ein Thema von J. Haydn für Orchester, Op. 56a," in *Johannes Brahms Symphonien und andere Orchesterwerke,* ed. A. Morin. Berlin & Vienna, [ca. 1903]. [A structural analysis in the genre of *Musikführer* (musical guides) by an important late 19th-century theorist and minor composer, and acquaintance of Brahms.]

Luithlen, Viktor. "Studie zu Johannes Brahms' Werken in Variationenform," *Studien zur Musikwissenschaft,* XIV (1927), 286–320. [The first and basic survey-study on Brahms's variations and variation techniques.]

McCorkle, Donald M., in collaboration with Margit L. McCorkle. "Five Fundamental Obstacles in Brahms Source Research," *Acta musicologica,* XLVIII/2 (1976).

Mies, Paul. "Aus Brahms' Werkstatt; Vom Entstehen und Werden der Werke bei Brahms," *N. Simrock Jahrbuch I,* ed. Erich H. Müller. Berlin, 1928, 43–63.

Nelson, Robert U. *The Technique of Variation. A Study of the Instrumental Variation Form from Antonio de Cabezón to Max Reger.* Berkeley & Los Angeles, 1948. [Includes historical analyses of the significance of Brahms's variation techniques.]

Orel, Alfred. "Skizzen zu Joh. Brahms' Haydn=Variationen," *Zeitschrift für Musikwissenschaft,* V/6 (March 1923), 296–315. [First study of the sketches.]

Donald M. McCorkle (b. 1929) is Professor of Musicology and former Head of the Department of Music at The University of British Columbia, Vancouver. Previously, he taught in the Graduate School of the University of Maryland. During 1954–64, he opened the music archives of the Moravian Church in America and established The Moravian Music Foundation, of which he served as director. He has published many scholarly editions of the late 18th-century music of the American Moravians, and a number of important articles on their musical traditions, composers, and repertoire, as well as essays on American music in general. Since 1964 he has devoted his research attention primarily to critical studies on the works of Brahms, particularly through the autograph manuscripts and original editions in the United States and Europe.

DATE DUE
